IT'S YOUR MONEY!

J. SYLVESTER WOOD

outskirts
press

IT'S YOUR MONEY!
All Rights Reserved.
Copyright © 2020 J. Sylvester Wood
v3.0

The opinions expressed in this manuscript are solely the opinions of the author and do not represent the opinions or thoughts of the publisher. The author has represented and warranted full ownership and/or legal right to publish all the materials in this book.

This book may not be reproduced, transmitted, or stored in whole or in part by any means, including graphic, electronic, or mechanical without the express written consent of the publisher except in the case of brief quotations embodied in critical articles and reviews.

Outskirts Press, Inc.
http://www.outskirtspress.com

ISBN: 978-1-9772-1582-6

Cover Photo © 2020 J Photography of Grand Rapids, LLC. All rights reserved - used with permission.

Outskirts Press and the "OP" logo are trademarks belonging to Outskirts Press, Inc.

PRINTED IN THE UNITED STATES OF AMERICA

*To my wife and family.
The joy of my life.*

TABLE OF CONTENTS

INTRODUCTION i

CHAPTER I: THE BEGINNING 1
    HIGH TURNOVER BUSINESS 3
    MISPLACED TRUST 5
    HIGH RISK=HIGH COMMISSIONS 7
    TIME TO MOVE ON 9

CHAPTER II: MONEY TALK 13
    GAMBLING 21
    A TRUE STORY 22
    SAFETY? WHAT'S THAT? 25

CHAPTER III: A BRIEF HISTORY OF MONEY 27
    BANKING 39
    CIVIL WAR EMERGENCY 41
    THE FEDERAL RESERVE 41
    DUTIES OF THE FED 42

CHAPTER IV: A BRIEF HISTORY OF MONEY
(CONTINUED) 45
    PAPER MONEY 45
    PAPER MONEY COMES TO AMERICA 46

THE CONSTITUTION vs PAPER MONEY 47
THE LINCOLN/CHASE AGREEMENT 49
THE WASHINGTON MONEY MACHINE 51
ELECTRONIC MONEY.......................................52

CHAPTER V: WALL STREET 56
   VOLATILITY IN THE MARKET 58
   THE GREAT CRASH 59
   THE GREAT RECESSION 62
   THE CASINO OF THE RICH 65

CHAPTER VI: RISK..69
   MARKET RISK. 70
   INFLATION RISK. 70
   INTEREST RATE RISK. 70
   SHORTFALL RISK. 70
   POLITICAL RISK. 71
   SOCIETAL RISK. 71
   RISK TRANSFER PREMIUM/RISK
   PREMIUM 78

CHAPTER VII: MUTUAL FUNDS 84

CHAPTER VIII: ANNUITIES 94
   A LONG HISTORY...95
   FAMOUS ANNUITY OWNERS 96
   CIVIL WAR ANNUITIES...................................97
   IMMEDIATE ANNUITIES 99
   LIFE ANNUITIES 99

DEFERRED ANNUITIES 100
VARIABLE ANNUITIES................................ 101
TAX-DEFERRED GROWTH 104
CAPITAL GAINS vs ORDINARY INCOME 105

CHAPTER IX: FIXED-INDEXED ANNUITIES 107
NOT AN INVESTMENT? 109
INFLATION, THE SILENT THIEF 111
THE CASINO 112

CHAPTER X: LEGAL RESERVE LIFE
INSURANCE COMPANIES 120
INSURANCE IN AMERICA 122
INSURANCE COMPANY RATINGS 125

CHAPTER XI: THE LIVING TRUST 128
WHAT IS A TRUST, ANYWAY?..................... 130
DISINHERITED CHILDREN 133
VERY UNHAPPY CHILDREN 134
TRUST MILLS.. 136

CHAPTER XII: THE LAST MILE 138
A RANDOM WALK DOWN WALL STREET... 142
SAFELY IN THE BANK................................. 146

EPILOGUE: A FINAL WORD 150
Luke 17:20-21 153

INTRODUCTION

I have been in the financial services profession for nearly four decades. I started selling life insurance (a tough job) in the early eighties. Eventually I went back to school to study finance at one of the most prestigious business schools in the United States. This opened a whole new world to me and took my career in an entirely new direction.

Over the years, I have read literally hundreds of financial books, some written by the brightest minds in the financial world both past and present. There is one thing they all seem to have in common, with a few notable exceptions, they are incomprehensible and unreadable for most people, even for someone like myself who has a degree of understanding of the subject matter to begin with.

This book is an attempt to rectify that situation. It will be a refreshing change for you if you have never been able to make it through a boring financial book. And, it will be a poke in the eye for all the "experts" and "financial gurus" who can't (or won't) speak the language of the Average American.

Among those "notable exceptions" referred to above, is a wonderful book written by Fred Schwed Jr titled *"Where Are The Customer's Yachts?"*. This title came from a joke circulating around Wall Street about a Midwest visitor to New York who, after seeing the huge yachts owned by some of Wall Street's richest stock brokers, naively asked, "But, where are the customers yachts?"

Mr Schwed lost a fortune in the great market crash of 1929 but retained a great sense of humor about it which has made his book loads of fun to read. His book was first published in 1940 and has remained in print ever since. It offers a look into the world of Wall Street that is as true and viable today as it was then. It is truthful and spot-on because Wall Street hasn't changed, only the speed at which it operates is different.

Since my book, like his, is an attempt to shed light on an obscure subject without putting the readers to sleep, here are a couple quotes from Fred Schwed's book that are relevant to both his and mine:

"There will be found in this work a scandalous lack of statistical proof. There will be no sentences beginning: *"In this connection it is significant to note that* *reliable figures compiled by a prominent school of business administration reveal that in the first quarter of 1938, $218,350,626.55, or 8 ¼ percent of the total income of families of four or more including at least one wage earner, but exclusive of any money derived from dividends or rents, etc., etc., etc."*

Here's another one that he clipped out of *The Wall Street Journal* and printed it under the almost laughable heading, "Market Ideas....":

"A leading brokerage house says; *"During the slow rise from the April lows which carried the Dow-Jones industrial average from approximately 121 to the 139 level, the action of the market was regarded as in the nature of a technical recovery with little thought of the imminence of dynamic action. Resistance, as expected, was encountered just under 140; but after a one-day decline, volume dwindled, and the market presently appears to be engaged in a somewhat hazy consolidation movement, and perhaps searching for dynamic forces which will encourage broad gauge buying and the resulting demolition of resistance barriers."*

Mr Schwed goes on to say, "If the thoughtful reader will now read that statement backwards, he will discover that its original lucidity is not impaired."

Today, the Dow-Jones Industrial Average ranges in

the tens of thousands, yet the constant drivel spewing forth from Wall Street, its promoters and its agents, remains the same. You will find none of that in this book.

Thanks for reading. I hope you enjoy and learn.

J. Sylvester Wood

CAVEAT: The information and calculations in this book are accurate to the best of my knowledge but not guaranteed. Always check with your own sources before acting on anything we have discussed in these pages.

CHAPTER I

THE BEGINNING

She was 83 years old the day I rang her doorbell on that clear summer morning so long ago. I was standing on the front porch of her small house in a working-class neighborhood of Grand Rapids, the second largest city in Michigan after the mega metropolis of Detroit. As I waited, I noticed the lawn was trimmed and well kept, as were the lawns of the other houses on the street. These were small homes built immediately after World War II. The American troops came home after winning "The Great War" to face a new challenge, to be fruitful and multiply, a task which they gladly took up with great enthusiasm and gusto.

The need for new housing to accommodate the happy results of the heroic efforts to meet that new challenge by those newly returned heroes was great, and the home building industry responded by creating millions of small, affordable houses all across America. The Veterans Administration, under the authority given by the "GI Bill," stepped in to provide access to billions of dollars in new mortgages with nothing down, low interest rates, and low payments spread out over thirty years. All these elements combined to facilitate the greatest baby boom the world has ever witnessed.

As I was reflecting on these things, the front door opened and the lady I was there to see introduced herself and invited me in. Stepping over the threshold, I saw that the inside of her home was as well-kept and orderly as the outside. Her face bore the marks of time, but her smile was warm and genuine. The plain, printed dress she wore was dated but appropriate for a woman at her stage of life. She was small, but trim, and she seemed to be quite fit.

The pictures on her living room wall told the story of her family. There was the deceased husband, dressed in a suit and tie and wearing a rakishly angled fedora hat, as was the fashion in his day. Several pictures showed the two of them as a carefree and happy couple in the early stages of their life together. In another picture there were her two sons and one daughter along with herself and four grandchildren. The absence of her husband in the picture suggested it was taken after his passing. There was a granddaughter, older now, beaming at the camera in her cap and gown the day of her graduation from the University of Michigan.

She asked if I would like some tea. Now, I have been a coffee drinker since I was a teenager (strong, dark roast, never adulterated with cream or sugar). To this day I can't stand the taste, the smell or even the look of tea. But I was learning to be a salesman back then, so I said "Why yes. That would be wonderful." I followed her into the kitchen, sat down at the chrome and red vinyl table, and prepared myself to pretend I was enjoying the disgusting stuff this kind lady was about to place in front of me.

It was 1982, my first year in the financial services industry. I was trying to establish myself as an agent for a major insurance company and I was doing house calls. It would be many years before I reached the point in my career where people came to me. Now, at this early stage, I had to go to them. Like all rookies, I was scrambling to find my way, grasping at straws, eager to make it in a profession that held so much promise but was so very difficult to get started in.

HIGH TURNOVER BUSINESS

Most people outside the industry don't understand that fully half of all the men and women who enter any of the financial services, insurance, stock brokerage, financial planning, money management, mortgage agent, etc., drop out within the first year. Also, ninety percent of those who survive the first twelve months are gone within the next three to five years. Entry to most of the services is blocked by difficult, often brutal state and federal exam requirements which weed out many aspiring candidates right from the start. It's a very difficult line of work to get established in, although it can be highly satisfying and rewarding for those who can last.

The lady I was "visiting" that day was a longtime customer of the company I had just started working for. She was what was called an "orphan" because her original agent was one of those who didn't make it past the first twelve months. Rookie agents are routinely assigned to these orphan policyholders. This is a way for them to have people to call on and it keeps the customers happy thinking the company hasn't forgotten about them. Veteran agents don't make these calls, they consider it undignified and beneath them.

The purpose of my visit was to introduce myself as her new agent, establish rapport and see if there were other services I could provide and thereby earn a commission. I didn't make any money that day, but what I learned changed my view of the financial services profession. It changed the entire trajectory of my career, and, as I look back some four decades later, I realize that it changed my life.

MISPLACED TRUST

Ten years prior to my visit, when she was in her early seventies, her husband died after a long illness and left her with a substantial life insurance benefit of one hundred and fifty thousand dollars. That was over fifty years ago and, if you allow for an inflation rate of just three percent, it would be worth over six hundred thousand in today's dollars. Now, I don't care if you are Bill Gates, (which, of course, I know you are not because if you were, you wouldn't be reading this book!) six hundred thousand dollars is still an awful lot of money. Certainly, enough to allow her to live comfortably the rest of her life and leave a nice legacy for her children as well. Sadly, that's not the way it turned out.

She was a very religious person. She attended church every Sunday without fail. She went to Bible study and prayer meetings every Wednesday. In fact, since her husband had passed, and her children had grown, her church had become the center of her life. She did not drink, or smoke and all her friends were members of her church. All her social activities revolved around her church. Her entire life was imbued with the comfort, and the promise of the life to come, that her church gave to her.

It so happened that shortly before her husband died, the assistant pastor of her church had decided to leave the ministry and try his luck as a stock salesman for a big, nationwide insurance/financial services organization. I certainly don't want to get into a legal battle with any big insurance company, so I'm not going to give you the name here. Let's just say that it liked to portray an image of being "solid as a rock." I think you can figure it out. Right?

So, of course, being so deeply involved in her church, she contacted the former man of the cloth and trusted him with all the proceeds from the loving legacy her husband had left her. As I sat there at her kitchen table that morning, I had to choke back the tears while she explained that all her money was gone. Not a single dime remained. She lost it all due to her misplaced trust in someone and something she did not understand.

Like most people, the former pastor-turned-stock-salesman didn't last very long in that business. After just a few months, he quit and moved out of state leaving no forwarding address or contact information. Eventually, the investments he sold her collapsed and became worthless. She was left with nothing. So, there she was, in her declining years, living on Social

Security and a small pension from her husband's former employer. To say it broke my heart would be a gross understatement. It hit me like a sledgehammer.

As time passed, I could never get that lady out of my mind. I stayed in touch and called on her several more times just to say "hello." She was always sweet and gentle, and for some reason (thankfully) she never offered to make tea for me again. I guess I didn't hide my distaste for it very well that first day we met. She passed away five or six years later.

HIGH RISK=HIGH COMMISSIONS

After a lot of research, I was able to find out that she had been sold a high- risk derivative of some kind which was based on a foreign real estate venture. Undoubtedly, neither she nor the ex-pastor had a clue as to what she was being sold. When the venture collapsed, the derivatives became nothing but worthless paper. An early example of the notorious financial shenanigans by big-time banks and Wall Street robber barons that nearly brought down the entire American financial system in the great meltdown of 2007/2008.

I also learned that the "solid as a rock" company had been cited by the Securities and Exchange Commission (SEC) and had paid a hefty fine for the misleading sales tactics they used in promoting the disastrous crap. And, get this. The salespeople who sold it to the gullible public made a whopping ten percent commission.

TEN PERCENT!

That means the former reverend made fifteen thousand dollars on that sale. Factor in a three percent inflation rate as we did earlier and that's over $65,000 in today's money! No doubt three or four times his annual salary from his previous profession. Then he disappeared to God knows where (pun intended) and the trusting widow was left to live the rest of her life nearly destitute.

Disgusting!

I am an incorrigible optimist. I think the glass is always half full and I do my best to see only the good side of my fellow human beings, as difficult as that can be at times. I like to think she was not the victim of fraud or deceit. I don't want to believe that the ex-man-of-the-cloth purposely caused her harm. You see, I understand how stockbrokers work. Almost without exception this statement holds true: **the higher the risk, the higher the commission** (You will do well to remember this).

He was a rookie salesman and his former profession bore no relation to the harsh realities of the business world. I'm sure he was only following the orders of his managers, who were following the orders of their managers, who were following the orders of their managers, etc. No doubt, he was deeply sorry for the suffering he caused that poor woman. Although, to my knowledge, he never did apologize to her or make any effort to contact her after he disappeared from the scene.

Perhaps he remembered her in his prayers. Again, to my knowledge, his supplications, if they reached Heaven at all, never resulted in any beneficial effects here below.

However, the bottom line is the fact that he DID cause her much suffering and financial hardship for the rest of her life. Whether it was accidental or on purpose is beside the point because the end result was the same. She lost her financial security for the rest of her life while he and his managers and their managers made a bundle.

Doubly disgusting!

TIME TO MOVE ON

I only lasted a couple years at my first company. I never got that poor lady out of my mind and I saw many, many other similar cases. Usually the salesman (it was almost always a man back then) and the company were the winners and the trusting customer was the loser. I knew there had to be a better way and I made up my mind to find it or get out of the business. I'm happy to report that I did find it and I'm still in the business!

In this book, I'm going to share with you some what I've learned in nearly forty years. If you will follow the precepts and strategies I'm about to outline for you, your financial future will be far more secure. You will learn how you can earn a solid, consistent, reasonable rate of return on your retirement savings while lowering or even eliminating much of the risk. You will learn a simple, easy to understand formula that will help you achieve age-appropriate balance between risk and reward to earn a higher rate of return while at the same time protecting what you've worked so hard for all these years.

You will learn about little-understood financial strategies that allow you to enjoy market-linked returns without market risk.

You will learn why most people would be far better off to own a simple, low-cost index fund instead of high-cost brokerage accounts and actively managed mutual funds.

You will learn how to lower, or even eliminate, the second greatest danger to your retirement savings after market volatility, fees and commissions!

You will learn the fascinating history of money, what it is, where it came from and where it might be going.

I realize I may be telling you things that directly contradict the advice you've been getting from your own financial adviser, or the talking heads on TV, some radio talk-show guru, or from the most dangerous financial advisers of all, your friends and relatives. There are many good, honest and trustworthy people in the financial services profession. But there are also incompetent and poorly educated advisers, commission-hungry charlatans, and out-and-out crooks (remember Bernie Madoff?). What you are about to learn will go a long way toward helping you recognize the charlatans and the unqualified "experts," and protect yourself and your family from them.

This book is not a scholarly treatise on macro-economics. As a matter of fact, it's not a scholarly book at all. It is not intended to be read by any true expert. If you are an expert, then you have no reason to read it in the first place! It is written for you, if you have never read a financial book before and don't intend to ever read another one.

It's for you if you don't want to be overwhelmed by technical gobbledy-goop and you are willing to invest a little of your time. I will speak to you in plain English about important subjects in an easy-to-read, non-challenging format. At least, that is my goal. How well I achieve that goal will be for you to decide.

All right then, let's get going. Let's start out by talking about that very, VERY important subject that everybody is interested in.....MONEY!

CHAPTER II

MONEY TALK

"How strange it is that a fool or a knave with riches should be treated with more respect by the world than a good man, or a wise man, in poverty."

Ann Radcliffe, 1764

Let's face it, shall we? Our world revolves around money. We simply cannot function in modern society without it. The more of it we have, the better we are able to live and the more control we enjoy over our own lives. And, as the above quote tells us, the world seems to offer its greatest respect and admiration for those who have a lot of money, regardless of where it came from or whether it was acquired by fair means or foul. The older we get, the more we realize that just about everything we do in life has a monetary aspect. We are destined to spend a great portion of lives pursuing, worrying about, and being involved with…MONEY.

The United States is supposed to be a classless society. But, can anyone deny that the poor, the middle class, the rich and the really-really-rich occupy very distinct strata within our borders? Aren't these societal strata nothing more than class distinctions with another name? As Shakespeare taught us in *Romeo & Juliet*, *"What's in a name? A rose by any other name would smell as sweet."* A modern adaption of that five-hundred-year-old wisdom would observe that class by any other name is still class.

Even the most casual observer will see that all societies, the world over, are composed of different classes of people. Mankind has always been divided into classes. Throughout history, class was usually decided by birth and this is certainly still true in much of the world today. But, unlike most of the rest of the world, we can all be thankful that for us here in the United States, there is opportunity, through the application of hard work and perseverance, to rise above the mere accident of our birth. And what is the essential tool which will aid us in accomplishing this very desirable goal? MONEY!

So, let's spend some time talking about this essential tool together. Just to get the ball rolling, I'd like to ask you a few questions.

First question:

> What is the number one financial fear we all have as we get older?
>
> Answer: Running out of money.

Thomas Jefferson once said, *"I don't worry about dying too soon, I worry about living too long."* If he were alive today, he would be even more concerned because people are living longer today than at any other time in history. Here are a couple of interesting statistics for you to consider:

> **The Economist Magazine reported that over half of all the people who have ever lived beyond the age of sixty-five, in the entire history of the world, are alive on the Earth today.**
>
> **According to an article in the New York Times, the fastest growing age group in America is from eighty-five to one hundred.**

Please read those statements again and take a moment for them to sink in. These are amazing statistics with deep and profound implications.

Consider this for a moment: In 1935, when Social Security began, the average American life expectancy was fifty-eight. This, of course, was one of the reasons the benefits of the program began at sixty-five, most people didn't live long enough to collect them! As I write this, in 2019, the average American life expectancy is a little under 79. So, if the same criteria for receiving benefits were in use today as in 1935 (life expectancy plus seven years), nobody could start collecting benefits until age 86! Is it any wonder Social Security is in big financial trouble?

So, the good news is: **YOU'RE GOING TO LIVE A LONG TIME.**

And the bad news is: **YOU'RE GOING TO LIVE A LONG TIME.**

Today your money has to last longer than at any other time in history. Are you prepared for that? If you are, good for you. But, if you're like the vast majority of Americans over fifty, you most certainly are not. One of two things is guaranteed to happen to you, either you will outlive your money, or your money will outlive you.

Which would you prefer?

I've had clients tell me, a bit tongue-in-cheek, "I want it to come out even." I like to tell them (also a bit tongue-in-cheek) that I can certainly do that for them if they will tell me the exact date on which they plan to die. Unless you have a concrete date for that unhappy but unavoidable event, it's important that you plan for the good and bad news presented above. Proper planning, with a balanced, age-appropriate approach to risk and reward, can help you plan so that you don't run out of money before you run out of breath!

Alright, next question:

> What is the most important thing money provides us?
>
> Answer: Security.

I like to add a second answer to this question which is "independence." Because one of the important attributes of money its ability to give us a great deal of independence. Independence to live as we choose along with the power to exercise more control over the major aspects of our lives. If you lived in France, Germany, Switzerland or any of the European countries that have cradle-to-grave social safety net programs, and you get older without money, you will still be cared for by the government. You certainly won't have much independence, but you will be given a basic degree of security.

However, in our society, in the United States, the degree of security and independence we enjoy in our later years is directly determined by the amount of money we have at our disposal.

Am I right or wrong?

Whether or not that's the way it should be is a question best left to the preachers and philosophers. You and I must deal with reality and the reality is just this, especially as we get older, money is absolutely vital to our ability to maintain our security and independence, to say nothing of our dignity.

Now, let me say right here that I do not believe money is everything in life. Money doesn't give us happiness. For most of us, happiness comes from our families, from our faith, from living a balanced, productive life. But, having said that, let me also say this; while money isn't everything in life, it is important and the older we get the more important it becomes. In nearly forty years as a financial professional, the only people I've ever met who say money isn't important are people who don't have any!

Oh, but wait a minute. That's not quite true.

There is another group of people who say money isn't important, those who were born with it. The born-rich have absolutely no understanding of how the rest of us struggle all our lives over money issues. But if you were born rich you wouldn't be reading this book. You have never had to concern yourself with the issues we're talking about here. Yours is a different reality entirely.

However, if by some chance you are one of those most fortunate of people, and this book has somehow come into your hands, please close it right now and set it aside. It is not intended for you and you are wasting your time reading it. As a matter of fact, if you will go to my website (jsylvesterwood.com) and leave your name and address, where you bought the book and how much you paid for it, I will refund your money myself... I'm serious. Do it right now. And, best wishes to you, my friend. Enjoy your life and never forget to be thankful for your blessings. It's too bad we all could not enjoy such good fortune.

Oh, there's just one more thing. Rather than simply throwing your book away, would you please pass it on to someone who might benefit from it? On second thought, you probably don't know anybody like that, so could you at least leave it on a park bench or something?

OK. Next question:

> What is more important as you get older, a high rate of return or the safety of your money?
>
> Answer: Safety.

This is a real no-brainer. It does no good to get fifteen percent one year and lose fifty percent of more the way millions of Americans did in the Great Financial

Meltdown of 2008. It is vital as we get older to make the safety of our money our primary concern and always try to achieve a proper balance between risk and reward. Actually, as you will discover in the pages ahead, the core subject of this book is "BALANCE BETWEEN RISK AND REWARD."

Last question:

> Should an older, more mature person have the same degree financial risk as someone who is older?
>
> Answer: OF COURSE NOT!

This is another no-brainer that is so obvious the question should never even be asked in the first place.

Here's a question for you that I like to ask in my financial workshops; "What's the real difference between an older, more mature investor and someone who is younger?" Several years ago, a lady in the front row immediately answered, "Wrinkles!" That may be painfully true for many of us but the answer I'm looking for is, "TIME."

If you're thirty or forty years old and lose your money, that's not good, of course, but you have time to make it up. If you're fifty, sixty, seventy years old or older and lose your money, what will you do? Get another job? What kind of life can you have on Social Security and a minimum wage income from a part-time job?

Here's an idea for you. If you lose your money when you're older and past your prime employable years, maybe you could move in with your kids! How does that sound? Scary thought, isn't it? Of course, there's the very real possibility that one or more of your kids has already moved in with you!

If you lose your money, you will lose your independence and the ability to control the circumstances of your own life. You may very well end up being a burden to yourself, to your family, and to society as well. That shouldn't happen to anyone and its unlikely it will happen to you if you will take the time to understand and apply the financial concepts you will learn in this book.

GAMBLING

There is something deep within human nature that causes us to be attracted to gambling. Maybe it's this tendency to be drawn toward danger and risk-taking that has helped us become the dominant species on the planet and to be at the top of the food chain. And, let's face it, we sure wouldn't want to be any place other than at the very top!

But should we be gambling with money we've worked hard for all our lives? Money that is unlikely to ever be replaced once it is lost? Should we be taking chances that we may lose our future security and well-being?

According to Webster's Dictionary, gambling means, "...to bet on an uncertain outcome."

If you can't be certain of the outcome, if you don't know what the end result will be, then you are gambling. Isn't that right? There is simply no other term for it. And, if you are gambling with money you can't afford to lose, you are risking your future security and independence. You're taking the chance you'll end up being a burden to others the rest of your life. Nobody wants that. Yet, that's exactly what can happen if you're not vigilant and careful about how, where and with whom, you invest your hard-earned retirement savings.

A TRUE STORY

Several years ago, I was standing outside the meeting room after one of my financial workshop presentations when a man who had attended came up to talk with me. He said, "I really enjoyed listening to you. What you said made perfect sense to me. I'm afraid I don't have much money, but I would really like to meet with you sometime."

He was a tall, well-preserved man in his mid-sixties, clean-shaven, casually dressed and soft-spoken. I liked him right away and said, "Sure. Of course. Stop in my office sometime and we'll talk over a cup of coffee." A week or so later he sat in front of my desk and told me this heart-wrenching story:

"After thirty-five years on the job, I retired in 2005 with five hundred and thirty-three thousand dollars in my 401K." He reached in his pocket and said, "Take a look at this." He handed me his most recent statement and what I saw nearly made my jaw hit the top of my desk. The current value of his account was twenty-three thousand dollars! His name was Tom and I felt a bit tongue-tied as I stammered, "OK, Tom. What did you do with the rest of it?" He answered, "I didn't do anything with it, Jack. I lost it all."

"How can that be?" Again, I was stammering. "How could you lose half a million dollars?"

He said, "When I retired, I didn't know anything about investing but I knew I had to do something with my money. I couldn't leave it with the company I had been working for and I didn't want to just stick it in the bank. So, I asked around and a guy I had worked with gave me the name of a stockbroker he heard about who was supposed to be really sharp. I made an appointment with him and he said he could double my money in five or six years. That sounded good to me, so I turned all my account over to him."

"The first year I did pretty well but in the second year it started to drop a little. He told me not worry because it was just a normal fluctuation in the markets, and it would come back like it always does. But then, in the next few months, I lost over a hundred thousand dollars. I took it away from him and gave it to another broker. It still kept losing so I gave it to a different broker again, but I just kept losing. After I was down to fifty thousand, I just put it in the bank. Now I've been drawing on it to help with living expenses and, as you can see, there's not much left. My wife has a good job and I'm working part time, our kids are grown and on their own and our house is paid for. We don't owe anybody anything, so we're going to be OK, but I wish I had just put my money in the bank and left it there."

As he was telling me this, my mind drifted back to that poor woman I met at the beginning of my career who lost her money in much the same way Tom had lost his. Neither of them should have had all their money in risky investments but that's what happened because someone they trusted gave them very bad advice (Remember, *the higher the risk, the higher the commission*). Later in this book, you will learn how a balanced approach to risk and reward will help avoid something like this ever happening to you.

SAFETY? WHAT'S THAT?

I said, "Tom, didn't anybody talk to you about safety, maybe keeping at least half of your money in bonds, annuities or some type of safety-oriented investment?" He answered, "I kid you not, Jack. The only time I ever heard about anything like that was at your workshop. I sure wish I'd known you when I retired."

"I wish I had known you then, too, Tom" was all I could manage to say.

There was absolutely nothing I could do for him. It broke my heart to realize that here was another trusting soul who was forced to live an entirely different lifestyle because of somebody's greed and incompetence. It would seem those brokers whom Tom and that gentle lady from long ago had trusted, were blinded by greed to the most fundamental danger in all investments, no matter what the prevailing market conditions might be, RISK.

Most financial professionals will tell you that U.S. Government debt (bonds and T-bills), life insurance annuities and FDIC insured bank accounts are the only investments that can be considered "risk free." Of course, ultimately there is always a degree of risk even in those well-known safe havens. I suppose the Government could collapse, life insurance companies and banks could go bankrupt en mass, and our whole nation could descend into chaos. Nothing is impossible, but for our purposes, and for your peace of mind, U.S. debt instruments, annuities from legal reserve life insurance companies, and insured bank accounts can be considered to be as close to "risk free" as anything can get.

Risk is such an important subject that we will be devoting an entire chapter to it later on. But right now, let's relax a bit and have some fun. Let's explore the subject I know you are interested in, no matter how old, how rich, how poor, how handsome or beautiful you are.....MONEY!

WHAT IS IT?

WHERE DOES IT COME FROM?

Let's find out as we examine the history of that wonderful stuff.

CHAPTER III

A BRIEF HISTORY OF MONEY

"There are three faithful friends; an old wife, an old dog, and ready money."

Benjamin Franklin

Money does not occur in nature. No version of it is found in the animal kingdom. Like language itself, money is a uniquely human phenomenon. After thousands of years, money has become the dominant, over-arching institution involved in nearly all human affairs in the Civilized World.

OK. So, what is money anyway? That may seem like a strange question to most of us. After all, we know what money is, don't we?

Webster's Dictionary tells us that money is *"something generally accepted as a medium of exchange, a measure of value, or a means of payment."* Right. But, do we understand what it REALLY is? Is it simply some slips of paper in our wallet or purse, or is it something else, something far more elusive and abstract?

Let's try a little experiment. Let's examine a twenty-dollar bill together. Take one out of your wallet or purse please. What? You don't have one just now? That's OK. Go get one. I'll wait for you….Seriously…. Set this book aside and go get a twenty-dollar bill before we proceed…………..

I'm waiting…………..

Still waiting………….

Got it? Good. Let's look at it together.

First, what do you see on the front of the bill? A highly stylized picture of Andrew Jackson, the seventh President of the United States. (Do you think he ever really looked that good?) Strange that he should be there, because he hated the whole idea of paper money. He had almost zero understanding of economics, and he absolutely despised banks and bankers. His refusal to renew the charter of the Second Bank of The United States is widely believed to be the major cause of the great financial panic of 1837. But let's not dwell on his questionable legacy.

Take another look at the bill.

Notice that at the top it says, "Federal Reserve Note." Let's look down and see if we can find where it states that its redeemable for gold or silver. In the middle of the bill, on the left, we see the great seal of the United States. Directly beneath that we get the assurance that this note is "LEGAL TENDER FOR ALL DEBTS PUBLIC AND PRIVATE." That's certainly a good thing. For added assurance and to help put our mind at ease, we see the endorsement of the Treasurer of The United States. Pretty impressive, but I don't see the redemption guarantee. Hmm. Look over on the right side, maybe it's there. I see the seal of the Treasury Department and below that is another reassuring signature, this time it's the Secretary of the Treasury. It's all very official looking but still no redemption guarantee.

Maybe it's on the backside. Turn it over and let's take a look.

OK. On the backside there's a nice oval rendition of the White House. It's a twenty-dollar bill all right, because it says so five more times in addition to the five times it appears on the front side. But do you see the redemption guarantee? No! Of course, you don't because it is nowhere to be found, not on the front or the back. This is just a piece of paper not redeemable for anything except more paper. But wait! Not to worry. Hovering over the roof of the White house is something maybe even better, the comforting words, "IN GOD WE TRUST." What do you think most people would rather see, a redemption guarantee or a statement of faith? Which would you prefer?

Thanks to Richard Nixon, American dollars have been nothing but "fiat money," meaning they are not backed by anything other than the good faith and credit of the United States Government, since 1971. We'll get into that story later, but right now, set aside the twenty-dollar piece of paper and let's see if we can shed more light on the question of what money really is and where it comes from.

Most people think they understand where money came from. It's a familiar story that goes like this:

In primitive times, there was no money, people just traded one commodity for another, we call that "barter." When people needed something they didn't produce themselves, they would have to find someone else who had what they needed and was willing to trade it for whatever they had to trade.

Now, it's obvious from the start that this system was very, very inefficient. People had to find a person who had exactly what they wanted and who, in turn, wanted exactly what they had to trade. And, if this wasn't difficult enough, they both had to want these things and have these things at exactly the same time! So, after who knows how many thousands and thousands of years, the concept of a "medium of exchange" developed.

A medium of exchange had to involve the use of a commodity of some kind that most people would want and would be willing to accept in exchange for goods and services. Any type of commodity would do as long as it was generally agreed that, whatever it was, it was universally acceptable as payment. And, whatever this thing was, it didn't need to be desirable for its own sake because it could be used to acquire other things that would be desirable. This thing then, whatever it turned out to be, would be what we call "money."

No doubt, many different commodities were tried but, over the millennia, it developed that the most acceptable "money thing" of all was metal, especially gold and silver. Why? Because they don't rot, rust or shrink, they don't require maintenance or get sick and die (as in cows, pigs, chickens, etc.). They are easy to transport, and they can be made into larger or smaller units. Of course, cows, pigs, and chickens can be made into smaller units but that would make your money a whole lot messier, smellier, and harder to carry around!

This is the received wisdom about where money comes from that just about everybody accepts. There had to be thousands of years of barter, and barter societies, before the development of money.

It all sounds familiar, doesn't it? It's an old theory of the origins of money that is so obvious even a child can understand it. It is a narrative that can be found as far back as the writings of Aristotle. It is even proposed by none other than Adam Smith in his seminal work which became the foundation of modern economics, *"An Inquiry Into the Nature and Causes of the Wealth of Nations,"* holy writ for all who study Economics 101.

Like Most people, Smith also believed that metals, especially gold and silver, would be the most logical choice after many other commodities were tried and found to be unacceptable for the reasons just enumerated among other reasons now lost to history. This idea remains, among amateurs and experts alike the world over, the conventional wisdom regarding the origins of money. It makes all the sense in the world, it is absolutely logical, simple, easy to understand and intuitive. There is just one drawback to this very obvious and logical idea, it is absolutely, completely, totally, **one-hundred percent wrong!**

Not a single scholar or researcher has ever been able to find a society, historical or contemporary, that regularly conducted its trade by barter. Here are some examples of what leading researchers in the field of economics and anthropology have to say about it:

> *"Barter, in the strict sense of moneyless market exchange, has never been a quantitatively important or dominant mode of transaction in any past or present economic system of which we have hard information."*
>
> American anthropologist,
> George Dalton

> *"No example of a barter economy, pure and simple has ever been described, let alone the emergence from it of money; all available ethnography suggests that there has never been such a thing."*
>
> Cambridge University anthropologist,
> Caroline Humphrey

> *"Economic historians have occasionally maintained that evolution in economic intercourse has proceeded from a natural or barter economy to a money economy and ultimately to a credit economy. This view was put forward, for example, in 1864 by Bruno Hildebrand of the German historical school of economics; it happens to be wrong."*
>
> American economic historian Charles Kindleberger

> *"There is no evidence that it (a barter economy) ever happened, and an enormous amount of evidence suggesting that it did not."*
>
> Anthropologist David Graeber

Stop and think for a moment. Let's say its 1755, you are a wealthy shipowner (pleasant thought) and you are about to add a new ship to your fleet. How much gold or silver will be needed to buy it? Are you going to load up a couple wagons and haul them down to the shipbuilding company? No. Of course not. You would buy your new ship in the eighteenth century the same way you bought your new car in the twenty-first century, with very little, if any, cash, but with credits and debits. Any cash involved would represent a fraction of the actual cost. Even if you did write a check for the full amount of your new Cadillac or Lamborghini (you lucky dog), the check was just a debit against your account at your bank which became a credit to the car dealer's account at his bank. There was no gold, no silver, no commodity of any kind involved. Money in the past was the same as money is in the present.

In the United States today, informed estimates are that only about ten or twenty percent of all financial transactions involve the use of cash. Money remains as it has always been, mostly credits and debits, recorded on clay tablets in ancient times, entered on paper ledger accounts in the recent past, and buried deep in the digital bowels of bank super computers in the modern age.

Money is not a "thing." It is an idea, a concept, it has no corporeal existence. A dollar is nothing more than a measurement tool, much like a yardstick or a ruler. It is a way to measure the value of something else. It has no intrinsic value of its own.

I could fill up the rest of this book on this subject, but I want to move on. Let's just agree on this: What is money? It is a social contract, an accepted idea that a certain thing has value and can be exchanged for other things of value.

This "certain thing" we're talking about can be gold or silver, certainly. But it can also be a piece of otherwise worthless paper with symbols and signatures on it that give it an official aura. Or, it can be, and most often is, credit that is transferred from one account to another by any of the methods mentioned above, or by entirely new methods yet to be conceived by the mind of man.

Still, we must acknowledge the fact that history shows us people and governments do tend to think of money as a "thing," and have hoarded gold and, to a lesser degree, silver as far back as records exist and, most likely, for thousands of years before that. Nations the world over keep vast quantities in vaults and heavily guarded sanctuaries. For example, in the hills of Northern Kentucky, at a tightly guarded military base called "The Fort Knox Bullion Depository," the United States stores nearly five thousand tonnes of pure gold, more than half of this nation's total reserves.

Because gold does not rot, rust, or deteriorate, the Fort Knox gold may have been mined hundreds or even thousands of years ago. No doubt, it has been made into many different objects and melted down many times throughout the years. Some of it might have come from the ancient gold mines of Africa or Asia Minor. Certainly, some of it came from the blood-saturated booty robbed from the Aztecs of Mexico and the Incas of Peru by the savage and bloodthirsty Spanish Conquistadors.

Many people regard this, and other hordes of gold held by the United States Government, as a kind of psychic security that backs up the dollars we carry in our pockets. Nothing could be farther from the truth. The gold held by the Government has nothing whatever to do with the American dollar. It is part of the wealth of the American Government, just like storehouses filled with agricultural commodities, oil reserves, military equipment, etc. They are not connected in any way to the monetary system of the United States.

As we have seen earlier, gold is no longer connected to the dollar. The gold standard came to an end in the United Kingdom and the rest of the Western World at the outbreak of World War I. As they have so often in the past, nations turned to the printing presses to finance the tremendous costs of war, dropping the traditional redemption guarantees that made paper money acceptable to the vast majority of people.

On April 5, 1933, President Roosevelt signed an executive order making it unlawful for Americans to own gold. Possession of coins, bullion, or certificates in excess of one hundred dollars was made a felony punishable by a ten-thousand dollar fine (at least a quarter million dollars in today's money) or ten years in prison. All gold redemption ceased, and the public was given one month to bring their gold to the Federal Reserve or to one of its member banks. The dollar was then redeemable for gold only between nations for international transactions.

The ban was finally abolished, and Americans allowed to own gold legally once again, forty-two years later in 1975. That was four years after President Nixon caused shock and dismay the world over by decreeing that the other nations of the world would join the American people and not be allowed to redeem dollars for gold for any reason.

Today, the gold standard has become a thing of the past and American "silver" coins for general circulation are made of base metal slugs with a silver-like coating. Even the lowly penny has been robbed of any trace of its former metal, copper. Yet, despite dire predictions of economic collapse from many of the world's foremost "experts," our economy, and the economies of much of the rest of the world, continue to function at greater volumes than ever before.

Doesn't this reinforce the idea that money is not a "thing"? It is not a commodity but an idea, a concept, an agreed-upon fiction. As long as all the players accept the fiction as truth, it will continue to fulfill its function as the grease that keeps the wheels of commerce rolling. Let's all hope and pray the players never realize that those wheels are being lubricated by a will-o'-the-wisp.

BANKING

With all this talk about money, I feel we need to take a few moments to look at those strange and stalwart overseers of our money and the machinations of the financial world, those inscrutable institutions whose functions are so fundamental to modern society yet are so misunderstood by the vast majority of otherwise well-informed Americans, BANKS.

Banks and banking are ancient institutions, indeed. There is archeological evidence of lenders based in temples in Greece and Rome making loans and accepting deposits, in addition to money-changing activities, as long as four thousand years ago.

In the United States, after the American colonies won freedom from Britain, banks were chartered by the states and each was allowed to issue its own currency. (Can you imagine that?) The Founding Fathers realized the new nation would fail without a single financial system common to all the states. Alexander Hamilton influenced the creation of a centralized institution patterned after the powerful Bank of England. Founded in 1694 to act as the English government's banker, this venerable institution is still "THE BANK", even among economic scholars of today.

The First Bank of the United States opened in Philadelphia in 1791. It had the exclusive right to issue the national currency and it eventually spread to eight additional cities. Despite its success, however, Congress, in the dubious wisdom of most Congresses, refused to renew its charter in 1811. States soon began operating their own banks and issuing their own currency once again and, of course, the chaotic and inevitable results ensued.

When the War of 1812 broke out, the need for a central bank became overwhelmingly obvious once again and, with the intelligent and level-headed James Madison as President, Congress granted a charter for the Second Bank of the United States. This institution was even more successful than the first, eventually spreading out into twenty-nine branches. It, too, was to be short-lived. The cantankerous character we talked about earlier, Andrew Jackson, refused to renew its charter and by 1836 America's second attempt at a national bank had failed.

State governments proved to be woefully inadequate in regulating banks and by 1860 more than ten thousand different bank notes were in circulation throughout the country! When the banks failed and closed their doors, as many did, the note holders found themselves stuck with worthless paper. This, plus a new crisis that threatened to tear this nation apart at the seams, caused Congress to finally take action.

CIVIL WAR EMERGENCY

With the advent of the Civil War, Congress was brought, kicking and screaming, to the realization that the War would not be won without a national bank. President Lincoln signed the National Bank Act into law in 1864. The new legislation allowed individual banks to receive charters at either the national or the state level. National banks were required to use government-issued currency which was backed by United States Government bonds. Eventually, the state-chartered banks mostly phased out and since that time every bank in the United States has used the same government-backed coins and paper bills.

THE FEDERAL RESERVE

The central bank of the United States, called the Federal Reserve, was created in 1913 in response to a series of financial panics, mainly an especially severe panic in 1907.

Why is it called the Federal Reserve instead of the Central Bank of the United States?

That shouldn't be too hard to understand given what we have just learned about the historic animosity toward the central bank concept from the U.S. Congress. The bankers and businessmen who met on Jekyll Island, Georgia, December 23, 1913 to create an American central bank knew perfectly well it would never get past Congress if it was called a "central bank." Thus, they coined the term "Federal Reserve" or "The FED" as it has come to be called.

We observed earlier that in *Romeo and Juliet,* Shakespeare once asked, *"What's in a name?"* We've all heard the old cliché, *"If it looks like a duck, walks like a duck and quacks, its's probably a duck."* Well, if it looks like a central bank, acts like a central bank and talks like a central bank, it's probably a central bank. Let's have no doubt here, The Federal Reserve of The United States is the CENTRAL BANK of the United States.

DUTIES OF THE FED

According to its official documentation, the duties of the Federal Reserve (the FED) are "to conduct the nation's monetary policy, supervise and regulate banking institutions, maintain the stability of the financial system and provide financial services to depository institutions, the United States government, and foreign official institutions."

Sounds like a lot doesn't it? And it certainly is. The Federal Reserve of the United States, much like central banks in other developed nations, is one of the most powerful institutions in the world with the ability to affect the lives of millions of people through its policies and actions.

One of the unique aspects of the Federal Reserve System when compared to other central banks, is the existence of twelve regional branches located in major cities throughout the nation. These were created to give a regional perspective to the FED's activities and to offer a counter to the supposed Eastern bias of the home office, based in Washington, D.C.

The great market meltdown of 2007/2008, and the "Great Recession" which followed (more on that shortly), brought the power of the FED to the forefront as never before. Then Chairman, Ben Bernanke, led the charge that eventually pumped over eighty-five billion newly printed dollars into the economy every month in an effort to avert total collapse of the American financial system.

How successful was that historic effort? As we now know, the economy eventually recovered. How much of the recovery was the result of the FED's actions is the subject of intense debate among politicians and economists, their views usually heavily influenced by their particular political persuasion.

History has shown that excessive use of the printing press can, and usually does, destroy an economy along with the unwise government that runs the presses with abandon. It would seem that here in the

United States we have avoided such a fate for the time being. But, what about the next time? Or the time after that?

I would like to end this chapter with a quote from Thomas Jefferson, who was no friend of banks and bankers.

> *"The central bank is an institution of the most deadly hostility existing against the principles and form of our constitution…If The American people allow private banks to control the issuance of their currency, first by inflation and then by deflation, the banks and corporations that grow up around them will deprive the people of all their property until their children will wake up homeless on the continent their father conquered."*

As we have just observed, the central banks of the world are now the most powerful organizations in history. At this point, Thomas Jefferson's dire predictions have not materialized. Let's hope it stays that way.

CHAPTER IV

A BRIEF HISTORY OF MONEY (CONTINUED)

PAPER MONEY

The physical requirements to create paper money are really quite simple. You need:

1. Paper (well, DUH!), invented in China around 105 CE.

2. Fluid ink, also of Chinese origin from around 400 CE.

3. Block, printing, invented about 600 CE by Buddhist monks to help promote their religious doctrines.

But it is the very ease with which paper money is

created that makes it susceptible to abuse. Throughout all history, this been the Achille's Heel of paper money.

It seems governments, being composed of fallible men and women, can start printing money with all the best intentions and the highest degree of integrity. At some point, as economic and political pressures rise, they invariably fall into the trap of using the printing presses to excess. Inflation, loss of public trust, and often collapse of the government itself are the inevitable result**s.**

PAPER MONEY COMES TO AMERICA

The first American paper currency was created over 320 years ago in 1691. The Massachusetts Colony, having no other means available, printed "public credit bills" to pay soldiers and seamen for a failed expedition against Canada. Other colonies, both North and South, soon turned to paper money as well, often with disastrous results. Counterfeiting was widespread, and the most severe punishments were reserved for counterfeiters.

It is well known that the early Colonists were extremely antagonistic toward taxation without representation. What isn't so well understood is that they were equally as antagonistic toward taxation <u>with</u> representation as well!

Because taxes were nearly impossible to collect, and with no other options available to the Founding

Fathers for funding the needs of the fledgling Republic, the First Continental Congress approved America's first national currency, of which the initial printing was in 1776. These "continentals" were printed in such volume that they eventually became worthless, not even suitable for personal hygiene, the most humble use to which paper may be applied.

The phrase "not worth a continental" remains to this day part of the American lexicon.

THE CONSTITUTION vs PAPER MONEY

Article I, Section Eight, Clauses 2, 3 and 5 of the American Constitution reads this way:

> "The Congress shall have power...

> *"To borrow money on the credit of the United States:"*
>
> *"To regulate Commerce with foreign nations, and among the several Indian tribes..."*
>
> *"To coin Money, regulate the value thereof, and of foreign coin, and fix the Standard of Weights and Measures."*

The "power to borrow money" originally contained the line "to emit bills on the credit of the United States." This equated to a congressional power to print money. Several members of the Constitutional Convention, from both the North and South, moved quickly to strike that power.

What we see here are two separate and distinct powers allotted to the Federal Government by our Founding Fathers, the power to <u>borrow</u> money and the power to <u>coin</u> money. Even though paper money had a long history at that time, the power to <u>print</u> money is deliberately absent.

Some historians and many politicians insist the Founding Fathers understood the phrase, "to coin money" included the power to print paper money. However, judging from the historical record, no such power was intended by our Founding Fathers. Indeed, as we will see in a moment, it was only the pressing needs of the Civil War that ended, once and for all, the debate over the Government's power to print a national currency.

THE LINCOLN/CHASE AGREEMENT

President Lincoln and Secretary of the Treasury, Salmon P. Chase, needed to find a way to pay for an army and all the other monstrous costs of the Civil War. So, on February 25, 1862, with the endorsement of both Mr. Lincoln and Mr. Chase, Congress passed the first National Currency Act. It called for the issuance of one hundred-fifty million in legal tender notes. Because the reverse side of the new money was printed in green ink, they were called "greenbacks." The United States eventually issued a total of four hundred and fifty million in paper dollars during the Civil War.

The Confederate States, having lost the war, saw their paper money reduced to zero value, completely worthless except as a relic of an ill-conceived, unwinnable war. The Southern States officially authorized at least one and a half billion dollars in paper notes. Some estimates give the total printed far in excess of two billion. Allowing for just three percent inflation, that's over one hundred sixty-eight billion in today's money!!

In an odd twist of history, in 1870 the Supreme Court, with Salmon P. Chase Chief Justice, declared the issuance of the "greenbacks" by the Lincoln administration to be unconstitutional!

President Lincoln had appointed Salmon Chase to the office of Chief Justice in 1864 in a political move to remove him from his cabinet and get him out of his circle of influence. It was well known that Mr. Chase was convinced that it was a most grievous injustice, and a great loss to America, that he, who, in his own estimation, was supremely qualified for the position, never occupied the office of President.

By declaring the greenbacks to be unconstitutional, the Honorable Chief Justice ruled against himself. It was he who, in his earlier capacity as Secretary of the Treasury, along with the President, had approved the printing of those greenbacks in the first place. He even had his picture printed on some issues of the new bills to garner more public recognition during his upcoming (so he thought) presidential campaign. But, thankfully, in 1871 a new Supreme Court overturned that ruling, much to the chagrin and consternation of the dour Mr. Chase. He went to his grave in 1873 still convinced he was the most qualified man who was ever not elected President of The United States.

THE WASHINGTON MONEY MACHINE

Today, in Washington, D.C., at one end of Fourteenth Street, prostitutes and drug dealers openly ply their trade night and day. At the other end of the street, near the White House, the federal government prints money 24/7 in the workrooms of the Bureau of Engraving and Printing. They spew out Federal Reserve Notes worth over five hundred million dollars every day. These bills are distributed by the Federal Reserve in Washington to the twelve regional banks we talked about earlier. From there they are sent to the various member banks across the nation. Eventually, some of those bills, although sadly, not nearly enough of them, will find their way into our pockets.

Since the invention of the printing press, paper money has been used to replace bulkier, less manageable coins. In earlier times, when the paper was redeemable in gold or silver, the amount of paper money in circulation was limited by the amount of silver or gold available to back it up. Not so today.

In this modern era of "fiat money," governments are free to print as much as they wish, and they certainly do just that. Printing money is far easier than raising taxes or borrowing via the issuance of bonds. So, we can expect the various governments of the world, including our own (perhaps especially our own), to keep the presses rolling with happy abandon.

As we observed earlier, the words "payable to the bearer upon demand" have disappeared from our money altogether, and we are now obliged to be satisfied with the comforting words, "In God We Trust." As we end this discussion, I, once again, leave it to you to decide which is preferable.

ELECTRONIC MONEY

I have a confession to make, I LOVE INTERNET BANKING!

When I get paid (not nearly often enough), I don't get a check, I get a credit to my checking account. When that happy event occurs, I don't write checks to disperse those funds to the various places they need to go, I do it online. I love to go to my bank's website as I sit at my desk in the morning with my first cup of strong and black, dark-roast, wake-up coffee. I check my balances (Ah... Its still there!), maybe transfer some money to my bank debit card, or pay a couple bills. All done with a few clicks of the mouse.

Often, with more clicks, I pay on my mortgage, pay off credit cards, maybe make a contribution to my favorite charity or a deposit to my IRA. I make disbursements to various other places around the city and around the country. The "money" travels to its appointed destinations in a fraction of an instant. And it's all done most likely before my second cup of that powerful coffee!

I have never seen most of the money I have made the last few years. I have touched and handled only a tiny fraction of it. The fact is, I will never see anything except a small portion of what I earn. In the years ahead, I will continue to make money (hopefully), and I will see very little of it. I will never see it, touch it, smell it, or have any direct, physical connection with it. Most of my money is, has been, and will remain, just like most of the money the world over, INVISIBLE.

We are experiencing the age of internet banking and electronic money. Money itself has evolved to a few blips on a computer screen. Electronic money promises to expand the role of money in our society farther than metal, paper or plastic could possibly do.

This new money moves around the world without any corporeal existence outside the electronic domain. By moving at the speed of light, electronic money has become the most powerful financial, political and social force the world has ever seen. It has, in fact, become almost god-like, totally abstract, with no material substance, no physical presence what-so-ever, and its effectiveness subject solely to the degree of belief, trust and faith its followers have in it.

And there we have the most important terms in our discussion of the nature of money, "trust and faith". Without these two foundational building blocks, there would be no money as we know it. There would be no interstate expressways, no skyscrapers, no giant bridges, none of the trappings of the modern world. All the miracles of advanced technology and modern industry exist because you and I, along with the rest of society, have trust and faith in the money it takes to build these wonders. Money, that in and of itself, and without these two indispensable ingredients, is worthless.

We are now well into the era of fiat money, untethered to any commodity or anything of value. It is money simply because the issuing authority, the government, says it is. And just in case you harbor any doubts about the intrinsic value of today's dollars, read what the United States Treasury Department itself says about it:

> *"Federal Reserve notes are not redeemable in gold, silver or any other commodity, and receive no backing by anything. This has been the case since 1933. The notes have no value for themselves, but for what they will buy. In another sense, because they are legal tender, Federal Reserve Notes are "backed" by all the goods and services in the economy."*
>
> www.treasury.gov/resource-center/faqs/Currency

So, we see that money has taken a long and winding road to get where it is today. Whirling around the globe at the speed of light, seen only as a few blips on millions of computer screens, it has reached what is no doubt its final, finite essence. After thousands of years and countless iterations, it has evolved to become like the very wind itself, invisible to our eyes, yet wielding great power for good or ill. We know it is there because we experience its effects. Its existence is felt but never seen. Our money has now become......NOTHING!

CHAPTER V

WALL STREET

Now, let's take a look at the great American Stock Market, the playground of the "Masters of The Universe" (so they seem to believe!). Of course, the center of this universe is an eight-block-long street running northwest to southeast from Broadway to South Street, at the East River, in the financial district in lower Manhattan, in New York City, WALL STREET.

In 1624, thirty families disembarked from the Dutch ship, *Nieu Nederlandt* , onto the southern tip of Manhattan Island. The settlement they founded was named "New Amsterdam." Eventually a twelve-foot protective wall was erected at the northern edge of the colony. In 1655, English forces took control of the island and renamed the colony "New York" in honor of the Duke of York.

In 1685, surveyors laid out "Wall Street" along the lines of the original stockade or "wall." It became a gathering place for early buyers and sellers of stocks and bonds (a thriving industry in Amsterdam). By 1699, the population of the colony had spread far beyond its boundaries and, since the wall no longer served as a protective barrier, it was removed.

In 1711, the New York City Common Council made Wall Street the city's first official slave market for the sale and rental of enslaved Africans and Native Americans.

The opening of the Erie Canal in the early nineteenth century meant a huge boom in business for New York City. It was the only major Eastern seaport which had direct access by inland waterways to ports on the Great Lakes. Wall Street became the "money capital of America," a title it retains to this day.

Today, Wall Street is the home of the New York Stock Exchange, the world's largest stock exchange by market capitalization of its listed companies. Several smaller, although still important, exchanges have headquarters in the Wall Street area. These include NASDAQ, The New York Mercantile Exchange, and the New York Board of Trade. Anchored by Wall

Street, New York City has become one of the world's most important financial centers.

VOLATILITY IN THE MARKET

Throughout its history, the stock market has experienced periods of unfettered euphoria followed by severe downturns. The most famous of these downturns, of course, was the great crash of 1929. Before that catastrophic event, during previous market crashes, the word "panic" was the accepted term for the phenomenon. To make it sound better, government spokesmen and industry professionals began calling it a "depression" in an otherwise rising market. A nice, innocuous, non-threatening word.

"It's just a slight depression in the markets, folks. Nothing to worry about."

After the "Great Depression," as it came to be called, the word "depression," now much out of favor, was replaced by the less-threatening-sounding word, "recession."

Today, even that erstwhile, non-threatening term is in disfavor as we remember only too well the "Great Recession" that followed the market meltdown of 2007/2008. What new term or terms will come forth as politicians and their lackies seek a milder term to identify the financial downturns of the future? Stay tuned.

I recall watching a television news story some years back that featured a low-level government official who was being questioned by the press about a recent downturn in the markets. He refused to call the then-ongoing recession a recession, no doubt because of orders from his superiors. As he was pressed by the reporters, he became more and more flustered until he finally blurted out that the economy was in "a real banana." The news people laughed as did various audiences around the country. Fortunately, neither that term nor any of its fruity relatives has ever found a permanent home in the economic terminology of today.

THE GREAT CRASH

During the 1920s it seemed America could do no wrong. Our armies had helped end the "War to End All Wars" (World War 1) which devastated Europe but brought unprecedented prosperity to the United States. Our factories were at the peak of production and a new industrial age was dawning.

The great, driving engine for all this progress was the financial powerhouse of the world, Wall Street. Stocks climbed higher and higher as people bought shares in America's seemingly unstoppable success. This period was aptly named "The Roaring Twenties."

But then, the unbelievable happened. On October 28, 1929, the stock market suddenly crashed under the weight of its own speculative bubble. Terror struck millions of people as the ticker tape (computers were generations away) showed their fortunes melting away by the hour.

In that moment, the Great Depression began. Industries shut down, prices plummeted, businesses failed across the nation. The banking industry was hit with universal loan defaults. From 1930 to 1933, nearly nine thousand banks failed, impoverishing millions of people who were caught unaware and without recourse. It was a time of unparalleled poverty and unemployment in the United States.

On March 6th, 1933, President Theodore Roosevelt ordered that all banks be closed and declared a three-day "bank holiday." He promised the nation that the government would inspect every bank and only those found to be solvent would be allowed to reopen. To help restore confidence and stability, he leaned more heavily than ever on the Federal Reserve. Working closely with the banking industry through its network of member banks, the FED was destined to become all-powerful in matters of monetary policy.

That same year Congress passed the Glass-Steagall Act, which separated local or "retail" banks from the large investment banks, deemed to be the major culprits of the market crash. The Federal Deposit Insurance Corporation was created at that time. Once again, the goal was to establish confidence in the banks of the nation.

President Roosevelt did not restore money that had been lost by millions of Americans. Thousands of banks were declared unsound and never allowed to reopen. But thousands of other banks were found to be on solid ground and were allowed to go back to business. The crisis finally passed, and the United States economy limped along toward recovery until an event that shook the world brought it roaring back to life.

The Great Depression of 1929 remains the greatest economic disaster in U.S. history. For generations afterward, families would distrust banks and pass down stories about money lost and the incredible hardships of that era. The losses were massive. Stocks lost over eighty percent of their value and the markets took nearly twenty-five years to fully recover.

Many modern students of the era believe that it wasn't government policy that turned the country around, it was the events of December 7, 1941. That was the "day of infamy" when the Japanese bombed Pearl

Harbor and the United States' involvement in World War II could no longer be avoided. It was this event, the argument goes, that set the wheels of American industry turning at full speed and brought the greatest financial disaster in U.S. history (so far) to an end.

THE GREAT RECESSION

It's hard to overstate the magnitude of the great market meltdown of 2007-2008. Few people realize how close the world came to complete chaos and total financial collapse. Some estimates place of the loss of consumer wealth well north of fourteen trillion dollars! Venerable corporations such as Lehman Brothers in New York collapsed under the weight of hundreds of billions of dollars in losses. The most iconic corporation in the history of the United States, General Motors, required massive intrusions of cash from the government to avoid total collapse. Millions of Americans lost their homes to foreclosure. Millions of American jobs evaporated or were shipped overseas, never to be seen on American soil again.

Only the injection of nearly unlimited liquidity by the Federal Reserve kept some of the largest banks and businesses from going bankrupt and causing even deeper economic turmoil along with massive, unprecedented unemployment. It was, to put it in deeply understated terms, a disaster of monumental proportions.

What could have caused such a debacle? There is much blame to go around.

As we have just observed, in 1933, in the throes of the Great Depression, Congress passed the Glass-Stegall act. The purpose of this law was to separate banking into two broad categories, investment banking and retail banking. Investment banking means Wall Street and all that's involved in the buying and selling of stocks and bonds. Retail banking means the bank on the corner that serves the needs of you and me and the rest of the general public.

Glass-Steagall erected a wall between these two banking sectors to protect the public from the excesses that were a major factor in the crash of 1929. And, as we previously observed, as a further protection for average Americans, the Federal Deposit Insurance Corporation (FDIC) was established.

Confidence in the banking industry returned, the economy recovered, and the system worked just fine until Wall Street and the Big Banks started a massive lobbying campaign in the mid-1970s to eliminate government oversight of their operations and allow them nearly-free reign in their dealings with the public. Their efforts yielded rewards when they were able to get the Savings & Loan Banks deregulated in 1980.

How did that work out?

A little more than a decade later, over half of all Savings & Loan institutions in the United States were bankrupt. It cost American taxpayers over five-hundred billion dollars to bail them out.

You would think we would have learned that financial deregulation doesn't work, wouldn't you? Well, you would be wrong.

In 1999, after hundreds of millions of lobbying dollars and overt and covert greasing of Congressional palms, the Glass-Steagall Act was finally repealed. The banking industry was free to take the kind of huge risks that previously were disallowed under the protective provisions of the act. And this they did with almost no oversight from government regulatory agencies.

Repeal of Glass-Steagall and lack of government oversight were two major factors in the financial collapse of 2007/2008. Credit rating agencies, with high fees for their top-tier ratings at stake, failed to properly evaluate the risk inherent in new, highly lucrative, risky and complex financial products developed and promoted by the big investment banks. The bursting of the housing bubble was the last straw that finally brought the financial markets of the United States and the rest of the developed world to a standstill. From there the greatest financial disaster since 1929 descended on the world.

Can it happen again? Of course it can. And it almost certainly will. Why? Because people always want to believe that "this time is different." It never is really different. Only the circumstances and the financial instruments involved in the crisis will ever change. People, and human nature itself, never change.

As my all-time favorite economist, who could actually make economics fun to read, the late, great John Kenneth Galbraith has truthfully said in his wonderful book, "Money, Whence it Came, Where it Went":

> *"There can be few fields of human endeavor in which history counts for so little as in the world of finance. Past experience, to the extent that it is part of memory at all, is dismissed as the primitive refuge of those who do not have insight to the incredible wonders of the present."*

RIP Doctor Galbraith. I guess we will never learn.

THE CASINO OF THE RICH

Each day, over one hundred and fifty million shares are traded on the New York Stock Exchange for a combined value of over one hundred and seventy billion dollars! Where does all this money go? An exhaustive study by New York University economist Edward N. Wolf, published in 2016, gives us an interesting look into what the stock market means for most of the American people. According to this study, the top ten percent of American households, as defined by total wealth, now own eighty four percent of all stocks.

Furthermore, while ninety four percent of the very rich reported having significant stock holdings, only about twenty seven percent of the middle class hold any stocks at all. This tells us what we should already have known, Wall Street is not Main Street. Most Americans simply don't own stocks and all those gains in the markets we read about and hear about on TV are going mostly to the rich and the really-really rich.

And where does all this leave you, me and the millions of Americans who are neither rich nor poor but fall somewhere in the middle? Should we continue to miss out on the benefits of capitalism which seem to accrue only to the rich, the clever and the mendacious? I don't think so.

The information I'm about to share with you in the rest of this book should convince you that you, too, can and should enjoy the benefits of participation in the great American capitalist machine. I will show you how to do this and still avoid the devastating fate of catastrophic loss when the markets come tumbling down. And, let's all agree on this historically proven fact, shall we? Markets have always come tumbling down sooner or later in the past, and they will most surely do so again, and again, and again in the future. It's never a matter of "if". It's always a matter of "when".

When will they tumble? I don't know and neither does anyone else. If I were privy to such information, I wouldn't be here, writing this book in my office on a cold, snowy winter's day in Grand Rapids, Michigan. Instead, I would be writing it from the deck of my yacht in the Bahamas, or while relaxing poolside at the Waikiki Hilton, or maybe sipping rum drinks by the beach on the French Riviera. I'd be any place that's warmer, sunnier, and more hospitable than here!

OK. All silliness aside, history shows us that the markets are a reflection of the ebb and flow of human behavior. Humans, as we all know so very well, are the most irrational of all God's creatures. Their behavior is as unpredictable as it is unfathomable. The markets, being bound to human behavior like a cantankerous Siamese twin, are equally unpredictable and unfathomable. If we choose to participate in them, there is no escaping the volatile behavior they constantly exhibit. Therefore, we must protect ourselves if we are not to be overwhelmed or even destroyed by these untrustworthy forces. The key is to be prepared.

The very first stepping stone for us on this long and winding financial road, is to gain an understanding of, and get a handle on, that most important but least understood factor that you must deal with if you are to build and maintain financial security……RISK.

CHAPTER VI
RISK

"The biggest mistake made by most small investors is failure to assess and manage risk."

John Bogle Founder, Vanguard Funds

SEE NO RISK   HEAR NO RISK   SPEAK NO RISK

If you 're like most people, this is how you deal with risk!

Most people simply don't want to think about it. They think it's just too complicated for the average person to understand. And yet, it is simply THE most important thing we must consider when we evaluate any type of investment, large or small. You must always ask, "How much risk is involved", and, "Can I absorb the loss if I lose some or all of my money?"

Risk, simply defined, is the possibility of loss or injury. Investment risk is the possibility that an investment, such as stocks, bonds, mutual funds, real estate, commodities, etc., will lose value. There are many different kinds of investment risk and we need to take a look at some of them before we proceed:

MARKET RISK.

Or, "principal risk" is the chance that a market downturn, or just a bad investment, will eat up your money.

INFLATION RISK.

Or, "purchasing-power risk". The risk that your money won't grow fast enough to keep up with inflation and will be worth less and less with each passing year.

INTEREST RATE RISK.

If you tie your money up in a long-term investment at a certain interest rate, you take the chance that rates will go up and you will be stuck with a below-market rate of return.

SHORTFALL RISK.

This is the risk that you won't have enough money to reach your long-term goals by being either too conservative or too aggressive.

POLITICAL RISK.

This is the risk that government decisions will damage the value of your investments. Tax-law changes, international treaty agreements (or disagreements), changes in Social Security, or any number of political decisions can have an impact on your retirement savings, especially after you retire and no longer have employment-related income.

SOCIETAL RISK.

The risk of the ultra-big picture. This is what might impact your investments in case of terrorist attacks, war, natural disasters, etc.

For our purposes, and for the rest of this book, when I speak of risk, I'm referring to market risk. And traditional financial theory breaks market risk into two broad categories, SYSTEMATIC RISK and UN-SYSTEMATIC RISK.

Systematic risk is what comes from the "system" itself. When the markets take a nosedive, and stocks lose value, the financial system itself is the culprit. This type of risk is not subject to being lowered through diversification. During the great market meltdown of 2007/2008, when there was a fifty-three percent drop in the Standard & Poor's 500 index, it didn't matter how well diversified you were. If you were in the market, you lost! And most people lost big time. It was a textbook example of systematic risk.

Un-systematic, or business, risk is the risk that the particular stock you are invested in loses value even though the overall market may be unaffected. For example, you bought ten thousand shares of XYZ company because you thought it was going to go up like a balloon but instead it drops like a rock because of bad management, or changes in product demand, or other factors. A great recent example is the upheaval in the retail markets when online sales took off. Not a good time to have been invested in Sears, or J.C. Penny! This type of risk can be lowered through diversification.

Whether you are investing for your retirement or for more immediate needs, there are really only three things that can keep you from achieving your goals, inflation, taxes, and risk. You can plan for inflation and you can do a lot to avoid or reduce taxes, but risk is a horse of a different color because it is completely unpredictable. Yet, the results themselves are always predictable, you lose some or all your money.

We do not live in a risk-free society. There is simply no way to eliminate all risk, but there are strategies for dealing with this ever-present, dark anomaly that hangs over us at all times. Let's examine some basic risk management strategies. There are no theories or mathematical formulas here, no actuarial mumbo-jumbo. These are just some common sense, plain English approaches to this vitally important subject that most people don't want to think about.

Strategy Number One:

>Avoid the risk.

If you are thinking about taking a trip but worried the plane might crash, then don't fly. If you're thinking about investing but worried the market will crash, then don't invest. Avoid the risk entirely by not getting involved in the first place.

Strategy Number Two:

>Lower the risk.

Are you concerned about your health? You can lower

your risk with the two most hated words in the English language, diet and exercise. Although it's a slight digression, here's an illustration from my past:

I was a professional musician in my twenties and early thirties, before I made my father happy by going back to college and then getting a "real job." Back then there was an old musician's joke going around that went like this:

> *"There was this guy walking down the street in New York City carrying a violin case under his arm. He stopped a passerby and said "Excuse me. Can you tell me how to get to Carnegie Hall?" "Why, certainly," came the reply. "Practice my friend, practice."*

If he had asked that same person *"Can you tell me how to maintain my health and well-being?"* The reply would have been *"Why, certainly. Diet and exercise, my friend. Diet and exercise."*

It's one of those "common knowledge" things that everybody knows.

Are you concerned about market losses? It's "common knowledge" that you can lower your risk by diversifying.

Diversification is the classic way to reduce or lower

the risk involved in all investments. By combining assets into a portfolio of various stocks from different industries and different business sectors, you lower the overall risk of the group as a whole. This is your stockbroker's answer to risk. He or she will tell you that a well-diversified portfolio will lower your risk, and that is absolutely correct. But here's the kicker:

DIVERSIFICATION DOES NOT AND CANNOT ELIMINATE RISK.

Attempting to control market risk by diversification will help to reduce the risk but will not eliminate it. A major bear market, as we saw in the great 2007/2008 financial meltdown, can devastate even the most diversified portfolio. A rising tide lifts all boats, but a sinking ship takes down all who are aboard.

Strategy Number Three:

>   Accept the risk.

Every time you drive your car, you are accepting the risk of an accident. In the very act of getting out of bed in the morning, we are accepting the risks, large and small, that may await us. There is always a certain degree of risk in virtually everything we do. Let me give you a personal example of risk-acceptance from my own recent past:

A while back I had to do something that was really,

really tough. I had to go on a four-day, all-expense-paid business trip to…..Las Vegas! Oh, my, it was so very, very difficult (big sigh here).

I had to attend a Tony Bennett concert at Caesars' Palace, paid for by someone else. I had to stay in a three-hundred-dollar-a-night hotel suite, paid for by someone else. I was even forced to eat all my meals in a four-star restaurant, paid for by someone else.

Yes, indeed. It was rough.

So why am I telling you this? Not make you jealous (well, maybe to make you a little jealous) but to illustrate a point.

I got on that plane and flew to Las Vegas without so much as a second thought. I got on another plane four days later and flew home. Once again, never a thought about the risk I was taking. I simply accepted the risk in the same way we all accept the risk every time we get behind the wheel of a car or get out of bed in the morning. We just accept it automatically, without a thought.

You can do the same thing when you invest your hard-earned retirement savings. Invest it all in stocks or mutual funds and accept the risk. Maybe you'll get lucky. Maybe there will never be another market crash and you'll retire rich and comfortable. Maybe you'll laugh all the way to the bank at all those silly people who worried about losing their money in a market downturn and refused to take big risks.

Maybe.

But history does not support that idea at all. History assures us that sooner or later the markets always come down and very often they come CRASHING down. Still the choice is yours. You have the option of simply accepting the risk and seeing what happens. If you choose this option, I can only wish you well.

Oh, and you might want to start practicing for your new job which you will need if you turn out to be wrong:

"Do you want fries with that?" Or, "Welcome to Walmart."

Strategy Number Four:

>Transfer the Risk.

Do you have homeowner's insurance, or renter's insurance, or automobile insurance? If you do, then you are employing the concept of "risk transfer." You are transferring the major portion of the risk to an insurance company. You are giving up a small premium in return for protection against a large loss. The cost of the insurance is your risk-transfer premium. There are certain types of financial assets that allow you to do the same thing, that is, transfer the risk of a large loss in return for the payment of a small premium.

It is this concept of risk transfer that we will use later as we talk about how you can make your own financial future far more secure. One of the most popular risk transfer methods in the United States today is the use of fixed, indexed annuities or FIAs (much more on this later). This is a modern insurance product that allows you to participate in the gains of the market while taking no risk to your principal investment no matter what happens in the roller-coaster ride that is the American stock market. You can expect to receive a reasonable rate of return over time without risking a penny of what you've worked so hard to accumulate.

This type of investment is not appropriate for everyone and certainly not appropriate for all your investment dollars, at least not until later in your life. But, if used wisely, following the Rule of 100 (more on that later) and maintaining age-appropriate risk, it can offer a foundational strategy for securing your financial future.

RISK TRANSFER PREMIUM/RISK PREMIUM

"Risk transfer premium" is what it costs you to pass the risk to someone else. "Risk premium" is what you are entitled to for assuming the risk yourself.

By definition, all investments are accompanied by varying degrees of risk. Generally speaking, the higher the risk, the higher the expected return. (And, I can't emphasize this enough, generally speaking, the higher the risk, the higher the commission to the salesperson!) If you are willing to assume more risk, you are, in theory at least, thereby entitled to higher compensation for taking on that risk.

If you can safely invest your money in say, U.S. Treasury bills (assumed to be "risk free" because Uncle Sam can always print money to pay you) at three or four percent, but you choose something with an expected return of eight percent, the four or five percent difference is your <u>risk premium</u>. However, if, in this example, you receive just three or four percent (or whatever is equal to the return on the bonds you could have chosen) on the riskier investment, you have not been compensated for taking on additional risk above what you could have earned "risk free." You aren't earning any risk premium.

OK. So how can you know if you are taking too much risk? It seems that for something so important there should be some kind of measurement tool or yardstick as a guide. There must be a better way than just guessing or taking your stockbroker's word that its "low risk, nothing to worry about." Well, there is a simple, easy-to-understand formula that you can apply to all your investments which will help determine if you're taking on too much risk.

This formula was first suggested by one of my financial heroes, the late John Bogle, who founded the Vanguard family of mutual funds. It's called "Bogle's Rule" or, "The Rule of 100." It's based on the premise that you have a good chance of living one hundred years or even more, and your investment risk needs to reflect that happy fact.

Here's how it works. Take the number "100" and subtract your current age. If you are fifty-five years old, it would look like this:

$$100 - 55 = 45$$

So, the number fifty-five represents your "SAFETY RATIO," or, the percentage of your liquid assets to keep in safety-oriented investments. Conversely, the number forty-five represents your "RISK RATIO," or the percentage of your assets for more risk. Even here, however, these investments should be low-risk and conservative.

This formula, then, dictates that if you are seventy-five, no more than twenty-five percent of your assets should be at risk. Of course, there are many different degrees of risk, and many mitigating factors which should also be considered. That's another thing we will talk more about a little later. The important thing is that you understand the concept. An acceptable degree of risk at one stage of life can be entirely unacceptable at a different stage. This is the basic principle behind "age-appropriate" risk.

Another factor in using this formula is whether or not you are still working and earning employment income. If you are retired, I recommend you add an additional ten points or more to your Safety Ratio. Without income to help make up for possible losses, you need to be even more conservative

Over the course of my career, I have reviewed literally hundreds of brokerage account statements, put together by many different investment advisers, and brought to my office by people who were unhappy with their investments or just looking for a second opinion. Often, they had suffered losses they didn't understand, or, for various reasons, they were unhappy with their current financial adviser.

I can tell you this, in nearly every case, the formula for age-appropriate risk, was totally out whack or completely ignored altogether. Yet, had this formula been followed by the people who lost fifty percent or more in the great crash of 2007/2008, their losses would not have been nearly as great, and it would not have taken them nearly as long to recover. Don't let the simplicity of this concept fool you. It is a very powerful tool that anyone can understand and put to good use.

While I'm a big advocate of The Rule of 100, let me caution you that I still want you to be VERY conservative in all your investments. If thirty percent of your nest egg will be in things with more risk, those things should be low risk, age-appropriate, market-oriented financial instruments. Not, junk bonds, penny stocks, foreign investments, African gold mines, etc. We will talk about some low-risk alternatives a little later.

Earlier in this book, I told you the true story of "Tom," who lost over five hundred thousand dollars after he retired. If he would have consulted with me, he would have had at least sixty or seventy percent of his assets in solid, safety-oriented investments following the "Rule of 100." He might have had losses when the market crashed but a large percentage of his hard-earned savings would have been protected. The rest of his retirement years would have been entirely different, more comfortable, more enjoyable and more worry-free than they turned out to be. That is the power of the "Rule of 100" and age-appropriate risk.

Doesn't this make sense? Can you think of any reason you should not be using this concept to protect your own financial future?

Of course, this formula is simply a guide, not a hard

and fast rule (in finance, as in life, there are few, if any "hard and fast" rules). Many other factors must be considered, such as your own risk-tolerance, how much you can actually "afford" to lose, whether or not you still have employment income, etc. You also must be prepared to make adjustments to meet changing circumstances in your life.

Perhaps a medical condition will require reassessment of your financial plans. Maybe you'll have a rich uncle die or win the lottery (call me right away!). The important thing is that you make continual efforts to assess and manage your risk and make adjustments as changes in your life-circumstances require. The "Rule of 100" can be a life-long tool to help you be sure, as we've said before, you don't run out of money before you run out of breath.

CHAPTER VII

MUTUAL FUNDS

"Managers of other people's money seldom watch over it with the same vigilance...with which they watch over their own."

Adam Smith,
"The Wealth of Nations." 1776

"The mutual fund industry is now the world's largest skimming operation—a $7 trillion trough from which fund managers, brokers, and other insiders are steadily siphoning off an excessive slice of the nation's household, college and retirement savings."

Senator Peter Fitzgerald (R-Ill)
Government Affairs Subcommittee

Most small investors rarely buy stocks or bonds. They seldom buy gold, silver, or other commodities. Most Americans who have money in the stock market via their IRAs, 401(k) plans or other long-term investments own mutual funds and most of those people don't have a clue how mutual funds work. They simply don't understand what they own.

Since mutual funds play such an important role in the American financial landscape, I feel it's important that we spend some time trying to achieve a better understanding of what they are and how they work. Some of this is "heavy sledding" (definitely a Midwest colloquialism), but I'll try to make it as palatable as possible. I won't be offended if you decide to skip much of this!

A mutual fund is a professionally managed investment that pools money from many investors for the purpose of buying a diverse bag of securities. The companies that provide these investments to the general public are called "investment companies" or "registered investment companies."

Most mutual funds are "open-ended," which means investors can buy or sell the shares of the fund at any time and they are highly liquid.

All mutual funds in the United States must be registered with the Securities and Exchange Commission. They are subject to a detailed regulatory regime outlined in the Investment Company Act of 1940.

There basically three types of mutual funds in the United States:

1. **Open-End Funds** are required to buy back their shares from the investors at the end of every business day. The value of each share or, **net asset value**, (NAV) is computed every day. The price of the shares which the investor pays is the NAV as of the time of the sale. The total investment in the fund will vary based on shares sold, shares redeemed, and fluctuations in market value.

2. **Closed-End Funds** issue shares to the public only once, at the time they are created through an **initial public offering** (IPO). The shares are then listed for trading on a stock exchange and investors who want to sell their shares must do so through the exchange. The price they receive may be higher of lower than the NAV, resulting in a gain or loss on their investment.

3. **Exchange-Traded Funds** (ETF) are a fairly recent innovation. They are traded on a stock exchange, just like stocks or bonds and have become increasingly popular as investors are getting more and more comfortable with internet stock brokerage companies. An ETF can be structured as an open-end investment company, a united investment trust, a partnership,

grantor trust or bond fund. They have many of the characteristics of both closed-end funds and open-end funds. They are traded on a stock exchange at the current market price and, like open-end funds, investors normally get a price that is at or near net asset value.

Since most Americans buy open-end funds, and since the vast majority of mutual funds sold in the United States are open-end funds, from now on our discussion will concentrate on these types of funds only.

Although there many different classifications, let's just talk about the four main categories:

1. **Money Market Funds** invest in money market instruments which are fixed income securities with very short maturities and high credit quality. People use these funds as a substitute for bank savings accounts as they generally will offer a higher rate of return. However, unlike bank savings accounts, they are not insured by the Federal Deposit Insurance Corporation. While money market funds have lost much of their popularity since the Great Recession, they are still trusted by millions of Americans as a reasonable, short-term alternative to the low interest rates offered by banks. Low interest rates are a stated goal of the Federal Reserve

so we may safely assume this will be the case for the foreseeable future.

2. **Bond Funds** invest in fixed income debt securities, or what we call bonds. They are sub-classified according to the types of bonds they own, such as high-yield or "junk bonds," investment-grade bonds, U.S. government bonds, or municipal bonds. They are further classified by the maturity of the bonds held in the fund, short term, intermediate term, or long term. Domestic U.S. bond funds invest primarily in U.S. securities. Global or world funds invest in both U.S. and foreign securities, and international funds invest primarily in foreign securities.

3. **Stock or Equity Funds** invest in common stocks that represent an ownership share (thus the term "equity") in various corporations either foreign or domestic. There are two sub-classifications of stock funds:

   A. **Market Capitalization** indicates the size of the companies the fund buys. A company's market capitalization is equal to the number of shares outstanding times the market price of the stock.

   Large cap stocks have market capitalizations of at least ten billion dollars, mid-cap is from two billion to ten billion, small cap is below two billion and micro-cap stocks have market capitalizations below three hundred million. Mutual funds are also classified in these same categories based on the market caps of the stocks held within the funds.

B. **Investment Style** is the second sub-classification of stock funds. Growth Funds seek to invest in stocks of fast-growing companies while Value Funds seek to invest in stocks that appear to be cheap or priced below market value. Blended Funds try to reach a balance between growth and value.

4. **Hybrid Funds** invest in bonds, stocks, or convertible securities. Balanced funds, asset allocation funds, target date funds, target risk funds and lifestyle funds are all examples of the many types of hybrid funds available to the public.

Mutual Fund Expenses may be divided into five broad categories; distribution charges (sales charges and 12b-1 fees), management fees, shareholder transaction fees, securities transaction fees and miscellaneous other expenses. All funds must compute and publish an expense ratio which allows investors to compare the costs of different funds before making their investment. We won't spend a lot time discussing these various fees but the 12b1 fee needs to be explained.

12b-1 Fees are imbedded in the fund and are an annual fee meant to compensate the distributor of the fund shares for providing ongoing service to shareholders. It is paid by the fund and reduces the net asset value of the shares.

While there are funds which advertise as "no-load," that doesn't mean no expenses because "loads" are generally meant to mean sales charges. All the other fees will remain in place and cannot help but reduce the overall return to the investor.

Next, we need to consider how mutual funds can be divided into different classes. All classes invest in the same kind of portfolio securities, but each has different expenses and, therefore, different performance results. Funds can also use names such as Investor Class, Service Class, Institutional Class and so forth to identify the type of targeted investor.

Most funds that offer multiple classes identify them with letters. Typical share classes for funds sold through brokers would be:

Class A. Usually a front-end sales load and a 12b-1 fee.

Class B. No front-end load. Instead, they have a

high contingent deferred sales charge that declines gradually over several years in addition to the usual 12b-1 fee. Often, they will convert automatically to Class A after deferred charges have been paid.

Class C. Usually a high 12b-1 fee and a smaller contingent deferred sales charge for a short period of time.

Class I. Called "institutional shares," and will have a very high minimum investment requirement.

Class R. Designed for use in retirement plans.

Mutual funds offer convenience for the average investor but that's at a price. Fees and hidden charges can destroy your gains. For example: If you receive six percent interest in a given year but the maintenance fees add up to two percent, you've only made four percent on your principal. If inflation is two percent annually (the actual inflation rate can be higher), you are really only getting two percent, not much better than a bank CD. Add to that the fact that funds bought through a salesperson of some type (a stockbroker or "financial planner") will have a sales charge of up to five percent and you are better off keeping your money in the bank or even under your mattress!

When you buy a mutual fund, the agent will get paid, right? He may get paid in several different ways. For example, he might get an up-front fee of from two to five percent (Class A). He might get nothing up-front but collect a larger fee by spreading it out over several years (Class B). He may get a combination of the two plus "trail fees" which he will get every year for as long as you keep your account. The bottom line is that fact that he WILL get paid and YOU will pay it, in one form or another.

Fees and commissions will create a huge drag on your returns. For example, if you're fees are averaging three percent a year, on a $100,000 investment, that's thirty-thousand dollars over ten years! If inflation is just two percent (likely more), you need to make five percent just to keep even! And all the while the agent has been taking home a nice, fat chunk of your hard-earned money.

How does that make you feel? I hope it makes you upset.

But wait, there's more! To get the true picture, we must consider compounding and the effect those fees will have on your actual returns.

Compounded interest will make your $100,000 at 6% equal $179,084 in ten years. Sweet! But, subtract the 3% fees we just talked about and you have only $134,391 after ten years. That's $44,693 in somebody else's pocket instead of yours!

How does THAT make you feel?

Even if the fees were only 2% (unlikely), you will have $148,024 in ten years. That's ONLY $31,059 that you're giving away.

The key to a good mutual fund is low fees. Some modern funds, such as Vanguard, Fidelity, T. Rowe Price, among others, offer non-managed indexed funds with fees as low as .05% with no sales charges. So, in the example above, your return would be five and three-quarters percent. Over time, this can make a huge impact on your retirement savings.

Of course, the main disadvantage with all mutual funds is the same as with individual stocks, you can lose some or all of it! There is no protection when the market takes a nosedive. That's why using the Rule of 100 is so important. Put only what you can afford to lose in mutual funds, the rest in protected, safety-oriented investments and remember, the older you get, the more of your hard-earned money should be protected.

CHAPTER VIII

ANNUITIES

"It's not the return ON my money that concerns me; it's the return OF my money"

Mark Twain

Webster's Unabridged Dictionary defines annuity this way: *"ANNUITY...An amount payable yearly or at other regular intervals (as quarterly) for a certain or uncertain period (as years, for life, or in perpetuity).*

This is the classical meaning of an annuity, "annual payments." Today annuities have evolved into many different versions to accommodate the divergent needs of modern society. Basically, we can divide them into two categories, IMMEDIATE ANNUITIES, and DEFERRED ANNUITIES, those that start offering payments immediately and those that defer those payments to a later date.

Most annuities are issued by legal reserve life insurance companies. They can also be issued by many different entities such as pension programs or local and state governments for the benefit of their retirees. Private individuals can also offer annuities to other individuals. These are called, strangely enough, private annuities!

For tax-planning purposes or other reasons, wealthy individuals often leave an annuity (annual payments) to their heirs rather than a large lump sum. Trust departments at banks and other financial institutions are often chosen to administer such payments. These are examples of immediate annuities. For our purposes in this book, unless otherwise noted, when we talk about annuities, we will be referring to the deferred type, from legal reserve life insurance companies, rather than immediate annuities. The reason for this will become clear to you later on as we talk about ways to secure your financial future.

A LONG HISTORY

Annuities have a long and honorable history in the United States and an even longer history in Europe. During the time of the Roman Empire, annuities were used as compensation to soldiers for military service. Feudal lords and kings during the Middle Ages used annuities to help cover the costs of constant wars and conflicts. Popular because of the security they offered, European countries continued to offer annuity arrangements to pay for wars, provide for royal families and various other purposes.

In 1720, the Presbyterian Church issued some of the first recorded annuities in the United States. The purpose was to provide dependable retirement income to ministers and their families. One of the first to offer annuities to the general public was the Pennsylvania Insurance Company in 1912.

FAMOUS ANNUITY OWNERS

Some notable annuity owners include:

> LUDWIG von BEETOVEN. Received annuity payments established by Vienna social luminaries to keep him in the country. His benefactors supposedly felt that a man of such genius needed to be free of financial worries if he was to create his best work.
>
> BENJAMIN FRANKLIN. He left annuities in his will to the cities of Boston and Philadelphia. Incredibly, both annuities were still paying benefits to the cities in 1990, two hundred years after his death!
>
> BABE RUTH. From 1923 to 1929, the famous slugger contributed more than half his annual earnings, between thirty-five thousand and fifty-thousand (over a million dollars in today's money), to

annuities. His famous quote is particularly relevant to today's volatile and dangerous stock markets: *"I may take risks in life, but I will never risk my money. I use annuities and I never have to worry about my money."*

JOSEPH P. KENNEDY, SR. The patriarch of the Kennedy family was known to have deposited millions of dollars into annuities just before the stock market crash of 1929, thereby preserving his wealth for future generations.

OJ SIMPSON. It was revealed during the civil suit brought by his deceased wife's family, that he had placed over four million dollars in annuities. Under California law, this secured his wealth from lawsuits and creditors.

BEN BERNANKE. The former Federal Reserve Chairman disclosed in 2006 that his major financial assets were held in two annuities.

CIVIL WAR ANNUITIES

During the Civil War, annuities were awarded by the United States to military veterans. President Lincoln supported the plan as a method of assisting injured or disabled military personnel. After the War, President Grant disallowed many of these annuities because he was convinced the benefits were too high. The Supreme Court disagreed and restored the benefits to the veterans after a long legal battle.

Annuities today provide the same kind of benefits they have provided throughout history, safety, security and peace of mind that can come from no other type of investment. If benefits of this kind are important to you, using annuities as a central part of your long-term financial strategy, can be the best decision you will ever make.

For small investors, the most important feature of annuities from legal reserve life insurance companies is safety. All life insurance companies in the United States have guarantees in place much like deposit insurance for bank accounts. These programs are administered by the individual state insurance departments and mirror the guarantees from the Federal Deposit Insurance Corporation, currently two hundred-fifty thousand dollars in most states.

An even more important safety feature of annuities is the reserve requirements for life insurance companies. Reserves must be kept in adequate amounts to cover the deposits taken in for annuities. In addition, the all investments held by the company are highly regulated for safety. The fact is that life insurance companies have historically been the most trustworthy financial institutions in the world. You can sleep peacefully when you invest in annuities. Your money is safe and will be there when you need it. Or, if you don't need it, it will pass to your beneficiaries quickly and efficiently.

Now, let's have a brief discussion about these four different types of annuities, immediate, deferred and variable. We will discuss the fourth type, indexed, in the next chapter.

IMMEDIATE ANNUITIES

As we stated before, immediate annuities start payments to the beneficiary (the "annuitant") immediately. Generally, there two types of immediate annuities, period-certain and life. Period-certain sets up payments for a given period of time, such as ten or twenty years. At that time the original principal plus interest will have been used up and the annuity contract is ended. If the annuitant dies before the end of the contract, the payments will be made to his/her beneficiaries which are established at the time the contract is issued.

LIFE ANNUITIES

Life annuities guarantee payments for the life of the annuitant. This sounds great, doesn't it? Well, there's a catch. Let's talk about that.

The guaranteed payments are only for the life of the annuitant. So, let's say you establish a life annuity when you are sixty-five years old and your life expectancy is seventy-eight. If you live longer you will sock it to the insurance company which has to pay you no matter how long you live. But, on the other hand, if you die at sixty-six or any time before seventy-eight, the insurance company comes out ahead of the deal and there is no residual benefit to your heirs.

For hundreds of years, the life insurance industry has been collecting data on how long people live. This is a body of information known as "mortality tables." Out of say, one hundred thousand people of a given age and gender, they can calculate with uncanny accuracy how many of them will die in any given year. Of course, they can't tell which individuals from that group will die, but the larger the group being considered, the more accurate their calculations will be. That's why they can afford to guarantee life-time payments. Most of the people will not out-live their benefit period. Trust me on this, they know exactly what they are doing, and they always come out ahead!

DEFERRED ANNUITIES

A deferred annuity is exactly that, deferred. No payments are made to the annuitant until a later date when he/she decides to take them. Those payments can be made in any number of ways, monthly, quarterly, annually, or both principal and interest can be taken in a lump sum. This lump sum withdrawal is usually subject to a waiting period which can be up to several years in some cases. During this time, the original investment is increased through the accumulation of interest which makes deferred annuities popular for people who wish to set a given amount of money aside for future use or to pass on to heirs if it isn't used.

Here's a caveat (warning) for you: Be very careful about the length of the "waiting period" during which time there may be significant penalties for withdrawal of more than a small portion of the account (ten percent is generally the standard). This period can be up to ten years. I never recommend anything longer and prefer much less in most cases.

VARIABLE ANNUITIES

Variable annuities are highly complex. The term "variable" comes from the fact that the benefits can, and often do, vary. This is because the original principal deposit is placed in market-oriented investments so that the value of the investment will vary according to the vagaries of the market. In addition, there are generally high fees and commissions which might be OK when the markets are doing well, but they can be a major drag on the annuity when the markets are performing poorly.

In the interest of full disclosure, I must tell you that I'm not a fan of variable annuities. In point of fact, I dislike them intensely! I have never recommended them in the past and have no intention of doing so in the future. I feel there are lots of other options available that offer better guarantees, lower fees, and greater benefits to the average person who's looking for a safe place for their long-term savings.

I don't want to spend too much time on something I really don't like (can you tell?). But, here's what some other, better known, financial gurus have to say about variable annuities:

> "I hate variable annuities with a passion...especially variable annuities that are used in retirement accounts....I think variable annuities were created...for one reason only... to make the financial adviser selling you those variable annuities money...Just stay away from variable annuities and you'll do just fine."
>
> Suze Orman,

> "You rarely find me so deeply angry at a common investment Product that I dream of blowing it to smithereens....My target, Variable annuities."
>
> Jane Bryant Quinn, quoted in Newsweek

> *"High fees, low flexibility, and horrendous tax treatment make variable annuities less attractive than ever, except to the people who sell them."*
>
> Liz Pulliam Weston,
> MSN Money

> *"I cannot imagine a situation where I'd recommend a variable annuity."*
>
> John Biggs,
> Former Chairman of TIAA-CREF

One more negative thing about variable annuities is this, because your money is invested directly in the stock market, you will not have the protection of the guarantees provided in other types of annuities. So, to make up for this very obvious flaw, there is a built-in insurance plan to protect the account in the event of market failure. Great, right? Not so fast, there is a big charge for that insurance that puts another drag on your returns. Bummer!

OK. Let's not dwell on something so negative. Let me just say that if your financial adviser recommends a variable annuity, my advice would be to stand up, find the nearest exit, and get the hell out of there, FAST!

TAX-DEFERRED GROWTH

> *"Compound interest is the eighth wonder of the world. He who understands it, earns it…he who doesn't…pays it."*
>
> Albert Einstein

Benjamin Franklin also called compound interest the eighth wonder of the world, as indeed it is. This means you are earning interest not just on your original deposit but on the interest previously earned as well. Great! But even more wonderful is what I call "double compounding." This is what I mean:

All deferred annuities (even variable annuities, UGG!) offer a great benefit called "tax-deferral". When you have money in the bank, each January you will receive a 1099 form stating the interest you have been paid the previous twelve months (it won't be much!). This you must file with your federal and state tax forms. And, of course, pay taxes on that piddly little amount of interest you earned.

With a deferred annuity, you do not receive a 1099 form unless and until, you withdraw money. Because of this, you do not pay taxes on the interest you earn until its withdrawn. So, what you would have paid in taxes on your bank deposits simply stays in your account and gets compounded right along with the interest you are earning. This is double compounding...Fantastic!

If you are in a high-income tax bracket (lucky you!), this feature can be extremely valuable. It allows you to set aside a lump sum from your tax base, thereby lowering your overall tax obligation, while continuing to earn interest on your money and taking advantage of double compounding. If you make no withdrawals during your lifetime, the full accumulated value will pass to your named beneficiaries. They will owe taxes, payable as ordinary income, but only on the accrued interest, not on your original deposit. If your annuity is tax-qualified, i.e. an IRA, the full amount will be taxable to your beneficiaries, but they won't mind because they'll be getting your money. So what if they have to pay a few taxes?

Am I guilty of hyperbole if I call double compounding "the ninth wonder of the world"?

CAPITAL GAINS vs ORDINARY INCOME

Some critics of deferred annuities argue that it is a disadvantage to the beneficiaries of annuities to be required to pay ordinary income tax on the gains instead of the lower capital gains taxes that might be due from other types of investments, stocks, for example.

This criticism has merit to a certain degree, but only if the amount inherited from both investments were to be equal or nearly equal. The safety feature of the annuity, plus guaranteed minimum interest, means there **will be** ordinary income taxes to be paid. Such guarantees are not to be found in stocks or mutual funds. If the value of these investments were to be diminished, because of market downturns or business failure, most people would be farther ahead to receive the annuity and pay ordinary income taxes instead of a less valuable asset but one that is taxable at lower capital gains rates.

Let's move on now to a discussion of an investment plan that I really, REALLY like. In fact, I like it so much, and I have so much to say about it, that I will be devoting the entire next chapter to what I consider to be the greatest financial innovation since the creation of mutual funds, FIXED-INDEXED ANNUITIES.

CHAPTER IX

FIXED-INDEXED ANNUITIES

Traditionally, most small investors had two broad choices, stocks and mutual funds, or bank CDs and fixed annuities from life insurance companies. CDs and fixed annuities were safe, but they never produced much interest, often not even keeping up with inflation. Stocks and mutual funds might offer better returns, but they might also lose some or all the original investment, which they often do with gut-wrenching regularity.

In the mid-1990s, a new kind of investment vehicle was developed by the life insurance industry which aimed to fill the gap between these two traditional choices and offer direct competition with mutual funds. This was an entirely new concept, designed to capture a large portion of market gains without risk of principal, and it was destined to dominate the world of safety-oriented investments. It's called a FIXED-INDEXED ANNUITY.

Fixed Indexed Annuities, or "FIAs", have two parts; FIXED, the original deposit is "fixed", or guaranteed by the issuing insurance company, (There is generally a minimum interest rate as well.) and INDEXED. The total interest earned will depend on the performance of a stock market index, such as the Dow-Jones Industrial Average or the S&P 500. If the stock index rises, the owner of the FIA makes money. If the index falls, the owner doesn't make money but, and this is important, the owner NEVER LOSES!

As if this wasn't great enough, when interest is earned it is protected. At the end of each twelve-month period, the interest is permanently added to the principal (just like a bank savings account) and is protected from loss thereafter. And, we're not finished yet! Because it is a "fixed" annuity, it offers protection from creditors in most states, direct, no probate payout to beneficiaries, tax deferral on accrued interest, double compounding like we just discussed, plus the option to establish a guaranteed, lifetime income that cannot be outlived. WHEW!

After a major market downturn in the year 2000, investors were once again avoiding stocks and looking for safety. FIAs provided the perfect solution and sales jumped from over five billion dollars in 2000 to over twenty-five billion in 2006. But it was the great market meltdown of 2007/2008 that was the proving ground for this new concept in safety-oriented investments.

During the meltdown and the "Great Recession" that followed, when the Standard & Poor's 500 dropped over fifty-four percent and trillions of dollars of American retirement savings were lost, those who had placed their confidence in FIAs were protected from the ravages of the market. They didn't make money, but they didn't lose, and that was great. When others are losing their shirts and you lose nothing, you will love that zero!

By the time the markets recovered their losses, thanks to the Federal Reserve pumping hundreds of billions of newly-printed dollars into the economy, sales of FIAs had climbed to over thirty–seven billion and reached over one-hundred billion in 2017!

NOT AN INVESTMENT?

I generally use the term "investment" when I'm talking about FIAs, but I'm not sure that's entirely accurate. Placing your money in the bank isn't really an investment is it? There is no risk as long as it's under the FDIC guarantee, so it isn't an investment the way stocks and mutual funds are. Do you see the difference? All states have guarantee programs in place for life insurance customers. The guaranteed amount for annuities can vary from state to state but it is generally about the same as the FDIC. A Fixed-Indexed Annuity from a life insurance company is much the same as a bank account because there is no risk of principal if it is at or under the guaranteed amount.

As we discussed earlier, there is also an additional level of protection in FIA's which comes from the fact the all United States life insurance companies are required to maintain high reserves. Ratios of ninety to one hundred percent are common within the industry. Any company whose ratios fall below the requirements are subject to regulatory control by state insurance departments. Compare that to most bank's ratios of well under ten percent and you can understand why legal reserve life insurance companies are considered to be the safest financial institutions in the world.

OK, so if a Fixed-Indexed Annuity isn't an investment, what is it?

I feel a FIA is better thought of as a savings account you establish with a life insurance company, not an investment. It's a savings account with a twist, you have the opportunity to earn far more interest than you would in a bank savings account. You will make money when the stock markets are up but never lose money when they go down.

You have positioned yourself half-way between your bank and your stockbroker. You are taking advantage of an "investment" that fills a gap that existed in the past but no longer. Your FIA is like a mutual fund because your returns are based on market performance. Yet, it is also like a bank savings account because your principal is always protected.

INFLATION, THE SILENT THIEF

Let's assume you were one of the lucky ones during the financial meltdown of 2007/2008 and "only" lost maybe thirty percent. Now let's assume your losses were finally made up in just five years. Great! But wait a minute, what about inflation? If you had one-hundred thousand dollars invested, lost thirty thousand but had your hundred thousand back again five years later, you actually lost five years of interest plus, if inflation were just three percent, you lost over fifteen thousand dollars in purchasing power!

Inflation is a silent, ubiquitous thief. You cannot hide from it. It hovers over you like the Grim Reaper, reaching into your savings accounts, your investments, your pockets and even under your mattress to rob you, day after day, month after month, year after year. Your long-term planning must include techniques to beat inflation or at least stay even with it. Fixed-Indexed Annuities are an excellent way to battle this ghastly phantom without taking on additional risk.

Although corporate and municipal bonds are the traditional investments for fighting inflation with relative safety, in recent years municipal bankruptcies and corporate failures have shown us that these traditional inflation hedges aren't always safe and can't always be relied on. FIAs offer an excellent alternative.

Of course, if the markets never went down, everything we've been talking about would be meaningless, wouldn't it? We could all just put our money in stocks or mutual funds, sit back, relax and watch ourselves get rich! But, sorry to inform you, that just isn't the way the world works. We all know that markets always come down, sooner or later. It's never a question of "if," it's always a question of "when." Isn't that right?

I'm sure you will agree that human beings are nothing if not volatile and unpredictable. The markets are like a mirror reflecting that volatile, unpredictable ebb and flow of human activity. The more volatile the markets are, the more attractive the Fixed-Indexed Annuity becomes. It is, I believe, the very best way available to the average person to protect long-term savings from the ravages of inflation and the volatility of the financial markets.

THE CASINO

I am not a gambler. I have never deposited a single dime in a slot machine or played blackjack, roulette, craps, etc. and can't imagine that I ever

will. I have no religious taboos against gambling, as long as it's reasonable and not self-destructive. I simply have no urge, no psychological need, no burning desire, to gamble. But I have been in a few casinos over the years and have noticed one thing they all have in common... Invariably, as you walk in, you will see hundreds of slot machines. They are everywhere you look, sometimes they are even in the bathrooms. I will spare you any crude comments about that!

Why do casinos have so many slot machines and only a few gaming tables for cards, dice, etc.? Well, it's because slot machines are incredibly profitable. They don't need a dealer for each machine. They require very little maintenance. They don't call in sick or ask for a raise or maternity leave. They don't join unions or go on strike for better working conditions. They just sit there and wait to gobble up your money.

Actually, if the casinos had their way, they would probably have nothing but slot machines.

No, wait. That's not quite true.

If the casinos really had their way, you would just drive up to the front door, drop off your money, then leave!

They haven't found a way to get you to do that yet but it's a safe bet they're working on it! So, until they figure it out, their second choice will continue to be slot machines.

OK. Let's suppose you're feeling really good one Saturday afternoon, so you take a little trip to a nearby casino to try your luck. As you walk through the front door, of course, you see acres and acres of slot machines. But on this particular day, there are two of these one-armed bandits sitting side-by-side that grab your attention.

The one on your left is a traditional machine. You know how it works, right? You put your money in the slot, or maybe feed it your credit card information, pull the lever or push the button and watch those cool little wheels whirl around. You don't win, of course, so you put more money in and try again. You keep doing this for a while until you get frustrated, move over to another machine, and start pouring your hard-earned money into that one. Then somebody else sits down at the machine you just left, and on and on and on.

This scene is repeated over and over until finally somebody wins the jackpot. He or she then collects your money and the money of all those other poor suckers who came before and after you, minus a nice, healthy cut for the casino.

That's how a traditional slot machine works. Right?

But, let's suppose that on this happy day you have

some real luck because sitting right next to the first machine is another one that works very differently. With this machine, you can keep playing just as long as you want. You can play for hours or even days if you so choose. But, when you finally finish playing and are ready to leave, if you haven't won the jackpot, the machine will give you back all the money you put into it. You didn't win anything, but you didn't lose anything either.

Sounds like a fantastic idea, doesn't it? Quick, tell me where I can find one!

But we all know if it's too good to be true, there's got to be a catch, don't we? And, well, yes, there is a catch.

The catch is this: When you do hit the jackpot with the second machine, you will only get thirty, forty or maybe fifty percent of what the other machine would pay. Think about it for a moment. The odds of winning a jackpot are equal for either machine so:

Which one would you choose?

Would you give up the chance that you might get a bigger jackpot from the first machine in return for the guarantee that, even though you may win less, you will never lose anything if you choose the second one?

If you are twenty-five years old, you might go for the first machine because, at that age your hormones are raging, your mind is jumping around like a monkey on a leash, and you think you're going to live forever. You simply don't have the long-range vision and wisdom that (hopefully) comes with maturity.

But there is no need to talk about that because if you were twenty-five years old, you wouldn't be reading this book. That won't happen for at least another thirty years, or maybe longer.

If you have reached a later stage of life and you've acquired some maturity and wisdom, if your hormones are no longer driving you nuts, clouding up your mind and distorting your vision, unless you have money to burn, why would you even consider sitting down at that first machine?

I have a close friend whose wife goes to a casino two to three times every month. She loves to play the slots and she crows like rooster when she comes home a winner. She will talk about it for days on end. Of course, she never says a word when she loses, which I suspect is far more often than she wins, or that she cares to admit.

Wouldn't she be much better off if the occasional jackpot she wins were forty or fifty percent less but if she would always come home with at least as much as she left with? That way she could always brag that she didn't lose any money (because she is so very clever!) and brag even further when she did win.

Because her husband is a good friend of mine, I'm sure she will be reading this book and recognize who I'm talking about. I'm sorry Ann (not her real name) but, unfortunately, that second machine is totally fictional. It exists only in my imagination. You will never find it no matter how hard you look for it on your next excursion to the casino.

The fundamental concept behind a Fixed Indexed Annuity is that it is designed to allow you to participate in the great American capital markets without risking what you've worked so hard for all your life. It's like spending the day at the casino but always coming home with at least as much as you took with you. I believe this strategy should be a significant part of everyone's retirement planning, except for those who are so well off they're not concerned about losing money. But, as we've already discussed, those people aren't reading this book anyway.

What we are talking about here is the most innovative financial tool ever created for the average American. It offers unmatched safety while bringing the opportunities for financial growth to American families and retirees without risk of the devastation a financial crisis can cause. And, I've saved the best for last, all this with **NO COMMISSIONS AND NO FEES!**

What? No commissions or fees? How can that be?

When you make a deposit in an FIA from a legal reserve life insurance company, the agent will get paid, of course, but he will be paid by the company from their general fund, not from your deposit. If your initial deposit is $100,000, that's exactly how much will go to work for you. And, if you follow the guidelines, you will never lose a dime, no matter what happens in the roller coaster stock market. Most of the good FIAs also have a minimum guarantee, generally around one or two percent. This means that not only will you not lose anything, you are guaranteed a minimum return, something no mutual fund can offer.

Of course, it goes without saying that if you have a brokerage account, you are paying lots and lots of fees, most of which are cleverly buried out of sight in the account. You'll receive quarterly and annual statements that will give you some information about those fees, but you'll need a magnifying glass and a Philadelphia lawyer to dig it out from all the gobbled-goop.

One final caveat, however. As much as I like FIAs, they are highly complex financial instruments, no one should put their money in them without first talking with a qualified advisor.

Before we discuss how you will take advantage of the benefits of FIAs to secure your financial future, I feel we must take some time to examine where these modern financial wonders come from. They are available to you only from the most stable financial institutions in the history of the world, LEGAL RESERVE LIFE INSURANCE COMPANIES.

CHAPTER X

LEGAL RESERVE LIFE INSURANCE COMPANIES

Earlier, we talked about the fact that annuities have a long and honorable history in America and, indeed, most of the rest of the world as far back as the early Roman Empire. The term "annuity" comes from the Latin word "annus," which means "annual." Originally, it meant an annual payment which could be divided into any number of smaller units.

Cities, governments, kings, queens, and private individuals were among the early grantors of annuities. Often the annuity was given as payment for service, such as military service or an annuity left to servants in a wealthy person's will. Today, while privately funded annuities are still in use, annuities from legal reserve life insurance companies are the most popular and are what most people think of when they think of annuities.

The concept of life insurance goes all the way back to as early as 100, BCE when soldiers of the Roman

Empire formed burial clubs to pay for funeral expenses of other soldiers who were members of the club.

The purpose of these clubs was to pool the resources of the club members when a soldier died so there could be a proper burial of the deceased. The Romans were advanced in many ways, but the need for a proper burial was a little different than you might think. No doubt it was in line with the times for them to believe that if they did not get a proper burial, they would become miserable ghosts destined to dwell in spirit world limbo for all eternity!

This belief was so ardently held among the Roman people that the need arose for civilian burial clubs to assist the poor who could not afford proper burial. For without such, they could not avoid becoming unhappy, wandering phantoms of the underworld. Certainly, a miserable fate to be avoided if at all possible.

When a member of these civilian clubs died, all the other members pooled their resources and split the costs. That way even the poor could afford to help but no one had to bear the full burden of burial expenses. This idea is a lot like the concept of premiums, which was developed much later.

INSURANCE IN AMERICA

The first insurance company in the United States was formed in Charleston, South Carolina in 1735. Fire insurance was available first and life insurance was added in 1760. interestingly, many church leaders preached against it as something evil and wicked. They argued that buying life insurance was like gambling and betting against God. A sentiment that, fortunately, has been replaced by more enlightened understanding that providing for one's family is not offensive to God.

Life insurance did not become a mainstream financial product in the United States until one hundred years later, around the middle of the nineteenth century. It was then that insurers began appealing to the moral duty of husbands to provide for their families in the event of premature death (doesn't everyone die prematurely?). Some of the companies formed during that time period are still in business today, such as New York Life (1845), Mass Mutual (1851), Guardian Life (1860), and Metropolitan Life (1864).

A recent example of the value of life insurance to society was after September 11, 2001. Nearly three thousand people died in the terrorist attacks in New York and Washington. D.C., and the failed airline hijacking in Pennsylvania. Estimates are that nearly a billion and a-half dollars were paid in life insurance death benefits to the families of the innocent victims.

Why are legal reserve life insurance companies the safest, most stable financial institutions in the world? The answer lies in the term "legal reserve." To understand how the system works, we must first take a look at the way banks treat the subject of reserves.

Have you ever heard the term "fractional reserves" in regard to banks? It is the holy grail of the banking industry. It means a bank will keep only a fraction of total deposits in reserve to meet depositor redemption requests. It is also the biggest and most obvious cause of bank failures.

Fractional reserves were developed by banks centuries ago when they realized it was unlikely all their depositors would make withdrawals at the same time. This allowed them to make a lot more money by loaning out most of the deposits while keeping only a fraction in reserve to cover withdrawals, hence the term, "fractional reserves."

This all worked very well, of course, until all the depositors DID try to withdraw their money at the same time! This created a new and dreaded phenomenon, the run on the bank. When this happened, the bank was destined to fail, the banker was destined for the whipping post (or worse) if he hadn't already skipped town, and most, if not all, of the unhappy depositors were destined to lose some of or all their money.

As we discussed earlier, in 1933, President Franklin Roosevelt famously declared a "bank Holiday" to close the nation's banks and stop the banking panics that were sweeping the country. Why couldn't the banks pay back their depositor's money?

You now know the answer, don't you? Because of fractional reserve banking.

Today, there are federal and state reserve requirements which attempt to guarantee that banks will not overextend themselves. The late Nobel Prize winning economist Milton Friedman was among the many well-informed advocates of "100% reserves" for all banks. They argue that reserves should be at least equal to deposits. Many think reserves should be 150% of deposits or even more. Banks, unsurprisingly, tend to vehemently disagree. They typically argue that a 10% reserve is adequate and that anything greater will inhibit their ability to conduct business. Personally, I would much prefer they follow Doctor Friedman's suggestion. What's your opinion?

The Federal Deposit Insurance Corporation (FDIC), previously discussed, does offer a safety net to depositors but that is supported by taxpayers like you and me. As of this writing in 2019, the insured limit is $250,000. Compare that to virtually unlimited protection from the life insurance company reserve system and its obvious which institutions are the safest.

The reserve requirements for life insurance companies are established by the various state insurance regulatory agencies and can vary slightly from state to state. Generally, the requirements, called "statutory reserves," will be extremely high, particularly for annuity contracts. Life insurance companies have been issuing annuities from all the way back to the nineteenth century. From that time to this day, even during great financial disasters such as the Great Depression and the recent Great Recession, no annuity owner or beneficiary has ever lost a dime of their investment.

Talk about big business, there are over two thousand legal reserve life insurance companies in the United States. Collectively, they own, control, or manage more assets than all the banks and all the oil companies in the entire world combined!

INSURANCE COMPANY RATINGS

There are several rating companies that examine and rate the various U.S. companies. The best known and most widely published is A.M. Best, which has existed since 1899. It is a neutral, unbiased source that uses a lettering system that's easy to understand, such as A, A+, B, B++, etc. These ratings are readily available to the general public and can be relied on as indications of the stability of the company.

Obviously, the higher the rating, the more secure the company is considered to be.

The Legal Reserve System in the United States insures a level of safety unmatched by any other financial institutions. Today, the life insurance industry provides more than a trillion dollars of protection to the American people. Because of strict state insurance department regulations, the establishment of state insurance guarantee associations, the absence of fractional reserves, and the insurance industry's history of financial stability and public responsibility to operate in a manner beneficial to the welfare of the community, you can sleep well at night knowing your family is protected and your hard-earned money is safe.

I wanted to have this brief discussion of life insurance companies with you because in the next chapter I will be recommending that you place a large portion of your savings in annuities. Why? Because I don't want you to lose your financial freedom when the stock market crashes, as it always has and as it always will.

I want you to get a good, solid return on your investments without risking what you've worked so hard for all your life. I want you to outlive your money and pass a legacy to your family when you leave this world. The only way I can know for sure that these good things will happen for you is if you place your trust, your faith, and your money in the world's most stable financial institutions, legal reserve life insurance companies.

CHAPTER XI
THE LIVING TRUST

Whenever I meet with new clients, one of the first things I ask is whether they have a will or a trust. They almost always have a will, but most do not have a trust. When I ask why, it's usually because they don't understand trusts or have been thinking about it but haven't taken the time to get it done. At that point I encourage them to allow me to take their information and pass it on to our attorney who will decide if a trust is appropriate for them. Why do I always do this? Because I believe creating a Living Trust is not just good financial planning, it is also one of the most thoughtful, most loving things anyone can do for their family.

Throughout my career I have emphasized "safety" as the single most important financial consideration for anyone over fifty. Virtually all my clients, now especially but throughout my career in financial services, are over fifty years of age and most are well into their sixties and seventies. At this point in their lives, most are no longer employed or are only working part time.

This means the preservation of their money should be their single most important financial concern.

As I write this, I am in my mid-seventies. I enjoy near-perfect health, I love my work, and I expect to be able to continue to work and be productive for another ten years, perhaps even longer. However, I'm all too well aware that death is as much a part of life as is living. We must be prepared for both. The world got along just fine before we got here, and it will do just fine after we are gone. We should neither fear death nor seek it, for it will arrive at its appointed time for all of us no matter what our state of mind might be at that dreaded hour. When the ghastly phantom points its boney finger at us, there will be no escape and no delays. Dying is an unbreakable clause in the contract that exists between us and our Maker.

In our youth we don't consider such far away things. But alas, we are no longer young and such things are no longer far away, they are at our doorstep. We can no longer sweep them aside. An important consideration for people at this stage in their lives is passing their assets on to their families. And there is simply no better way to do this than with a LIVING TRUST.

But wait a minute. Isn't this supposed to be a financial book? Why are we talking about trusts?

This is a financial book, it is true. But it is mainly about preserving assets which have already been accumulated, usually over a person's lifetime. It's about preserving assets for you to use and enjoy during your lifetime, certainly, but also preserving them for your family as well. Don't you want your loved ones to be able to enjoy at least some of the fruits of your labor? The LIVING TRUST is the best way to do that.

But the reverse situation may also be true. Perhaps you do NOT want your family, or certain of its members, to inherit what you've worked so hard for all your life. Maybe you are in your third or fourth marriage and you fear your X-wives can't wait to go after your money in court, or that your current young wife may be all too eager for the opportunity to spend your money with abandon while cruising the Caribbean in the company of two or three even younger male friends. There can be any number of reasons you may want your assets protected from estranged family members, irresponsible children or grandchildren, revenge-crazed X-wives, etc. Once again, a living trust can be the tool you need to thwart the actions of those whose motivations may be assumed to be less than pristine and noble.

WHAT IS A TRUST, ANYWAY?

There are two basic types of trusts, *testamentary trust*, created after death by provision in the decedent's will, and *inter vivos trust*, created during an individual's lifetime. "Inter vivos" is Latin for "within or during life," hence the English term "Living Trust." A trust can be "irrevocable," may not be changed by anyone including the original creator (Grantor or Settlor), or it can be "revocable," changeable at the direction of the original creator. For our purposes, the only type of trust we will be considering is the "Revocable Living Trust" which for brevity's sake we just call a "Living Trust."

A Living Trust is an alternative to a will that you create during your lifetime. It allows you to pass assets to your beneficiaries quickly and efficiently, without the costs and delays of probate. The main purpose of probate is to change ownership in an asset when the original owner is deceased. In the case of a Living Trust, you do that during your lifetime, thus avoiding the need for probate. Of course, the process is highly complicated but that is the central idea and the main purpose.

Trusts can be created for an endless variety of reasons, but our focus is on establishing of a Living Trust for the purpose of:

1. Avoiding probate

2. Passing assets to beneficiaries with as few costs and delays as possible.

Your trust will not avoid taxes or protect you from Medicaid spenddown provisions, should that unhappy need ever arise. There are attorneys who draft trust documents purported to dodge taxes or get around Medicaid spenddown requirements, but these are highly controversial and of questionable legality, far beyond what we are discussing here.

When you establish a trust, you, the Grantor or Settlor, appoint a trustee for the trust, usually yourself and/or your wife, although it can be anyone you choose who is of legal age. You will name a Successor Trustee whose duty it will be to carry out the provisions of your trust. These provisions can vary greatly according to your own wishes. You may want all your children to inherit equally, or you may wish to make different provisions for each child.

Do you have a child whom you haven't seen in 30 years and who refuses to acknowledge you as parent? You may wish to disinherit that person entirely or have him/her receive a small fraction of what the other children receive. Is your oldest son addicted to alcohol or drugs, can't hold a job and living on the beach somewhere in Florida? Perhaps a monthly income from his inheritance with provisions for treatment and rehabilitation payments would be a greater act of love than simply dumping a lump sum of money on him.

I have been working with attorneys to provide Living Trusts for my clients for many years. My brother-in-law was a prominent attorney and was instrumental in helping me understand the need for trusts almost from the beginning of my career. Here's an example from my own experience that will show the power of a well-drawn Living Trust:

DISINHERITED CHILDREN

About twenty-five years ago or so, a client of mine who had over half-a-million dollars invested with me asked me to help him establish a trust to disinherit his two adult children, a son and a daughter, and leave his entire estate to his live-in companion of several years whom he also wanted to be his Successor Trustee. He explained he had not seen or heard from his kids in many years, had tried to establish contact which they refused to acknowledge, and they had spread vicious and derogatory misinformation about him to all who would listen.

I explained what a major decision he was making and wanted him to be sure he understood what he was about to do. He was clearly of sound mind and was adamant regarding his intentions. I took detailed notes, as I always do, and passed them on to our attorney for evaluation. The attorney approved his request and drafted the documents which were signed, witnessed, and notarized in my office a couple weeks later.

Fast forward about ten years and the man dies. Within a matter of days, I received phone calls from both the son and the daughter wanting to know when they would be receiving their inheritance. I can't say it broke my heart to tell them they were not beneficiaries of their father's trust and that I was not at liberty to reveal any further details. I explained that the trust was a private document, if they wanted to know more, they could try to get a court order demanding that the current trustee (the live-in girlfriend) open its contents to their inspection, something I've never seen happen.

VERY UNHAPPY CHILDREN

The son made a few whimpering sounds and hung up. The daughter, I'm afraid, was less sanguine and, using highly colorful language, proceeded to question the legitimacy of my birth. Not being satisfied with that, she then made very crude remarks regarding my relationship with my mother and suggested I go perform an unnatural act on myself. I maintained my cool and told her I understood her frustration and that she had every right to seek legal counsel. I also informed her that since the current trustee of her father's trust was now my client, I was legally bound to watch out for her best interests only. I never heard from either of those disappointed children again.

Now let's fast forward another ten years and the live-in girlfriend, my client, dies. The investments she inherited had done quite well and even though they had been her sole source of income, she was able to pass the bulk of them on to her son who, I am happy to report, is NOW my client! All this happened quickly and efficiently without the intervention of the courts and with just a few hundred dollars in lawyer fees.

This was an unusual case. Most of my clients have a Living Trust and most of the time their assets are simply passed to the children evenly. Occasionally, provisions are made for charities, often for a grandchild's education, sometimes a gift is made to a special friend, etc. Seldom are the provisions in their trusts as dramatic and divisive as the one I just described. But the point I'm trying to make is that such provisions can be a part of your trust. The fact is, you can make provisions for anything that is legal. In many ways, your trust is an extension of yourself which lives on after you die to be sure your wishes are carried out.

I'm not going to get into the technical aspects of a Living Trust here. Those things you can discuss with your financial advisor and/or your attorney. I would just like to emphasize that establishing a trust is an important part of financial planning and almost everyone with assets to pass on to their heirs can benefit from using a trust instead of a will.

TRUST MILLS

Here in the Midwest, and, as far as I can tell, in most other states, there are companies, called "trust mills," which peddle Living Trust services at exorbitant prices to an unsuspecting public. They always sell a "package" of services which includes a living trust and accompanying documents plus extra lawyer services, discount eyeglass and hearing aid services, etc. The trusts they sell are generic documents, not created for the specific needs of the buyer, and usually come in a large, eye-appealing package which can be impressive, but is mostly useless smoke and mirrors. These companies often concentrate on rural communities where the populations seem to be more vulnerable.

As if all of this were not bad enough, the real purpose of these companies, and their main source of profit, is selling you annuities and other kinds of insurance. Their representatives are simply insurance salespeople who are paid by the commissions involved which they split with the company. The "annual review" they always offer is solely for the purpose of selling you more insurance products. The Attorneys General in many states keep trying to shut them down but they are often able to skirt the outside of the law or are shut down only to resurface with a different company name.

Needless to say, these companies and these salesmen are to be avoided at all costs. Always deal with local, trusted professionals. You'll save money and avoid getting ripped off by scam artists and charlatans.

This brief discussion of a Living Trust is not meant to be comprehensive and complete. All trusts are highly complicated and should only be considered after consultation with a qualified attorney.

CHAPTER XII
THE LAST MILE

We are now about to travel the last mile in our financial journey together. This is where the rubber meets the road and we apply what we've learned to your  own real-world situation. The first thing you must do is make a mental snapshot of where you are right now; your age, your financial situation, your family obligations, your health, your long-term goals, etc. All these things will impact on the financial decisions you must make.

Let's take an example and see if it fits you. Don't worry if it doesn't because it is meant to give you ideas for application and modification to your own situation. First, I will assume that you are at least fifty years old, so let's begin with that assumption because if you're not, you shouldn't be reading this book anyway.

Let's just say you're fifty-five years old, you've worked hard all your life, your kids are grown and have moved out of the house (hopefully!), you enjoy good health and you don't plan to retire for another ten or fifteen years, maybe even longer if your health holds up. First, we apply the Rule of One Hundred and we see that fifty-five percent (your "Safety Ratio") of your investments need to be safety-oriented, as close to "0-Risk" as possible, and the other forty-five percent (your "Risk Ratio") can take on more risk but should still be conservative. I think I can safely assume you would not have made it this far in this book if you were not interested in being conservative with your money.

You already know I'm going to recommend that you place fifty-five percent in Fixed Indexed Annuities (FIA). We won't discuss which companies you should choose but be sure any company you decide on has an A.M. Best rating of at least "A" or higher. Your financial adviser will help you find the companies and the type of FIA that suits your needs. Just remember, if he or she recommends a variable annuity, leave immediately!

One other factor to consider is your bank accounts. Since FDIC insured deposits are safe, whatever amount you keep in these accounts can be considered part of the fifty-five percent Safety Ratio you are trying to achieve. For our purposes here, you can deduct those deposits as a percentage of your FIA deposits. And, of course, the great advantage of bank accounts is their immediate liquidity and only you can determine how much liquidity you will need.

OK, what about the forty-five percent that will be in your Risk Ratio? For most people that will mean mutual funds and selecting the best funds for your particular situation will not be easy. To make it far easier for you, I would like you to plant in your mind one term… INDEXING.

Even the experts can't beat the market, why should you?

There is an idea floating around which I'm sure you have heard. It's an idea perpetuated by financial professionals and online "experts" alike, that if you take the right approach, do the right amount of research, and put in the right amount of effort, you can pick stocks and beat the market. Nonsense. It just isn't true. Almost nobody, including the top professionals on Wall Street, beats the market consistently. And, on the rare occasion when they do, it is most often more a matter of luck than skill (or they're cheating!).

Only a tiny fraction of the thousands of actively managed mutual funds being sold to the general public are able to beat the market and then only by a small percentage, about 1.1% according to the Dow/Jones Persistence

Scorecard which tracks and measures fund performance. The chances of you finding one of these funds amid the thousands that are on the market is probably about the same as finding that proverbial needle in a really-really big haystack. And remember, these funds are managed by people who devote their entire lives to this. They are smart, well-educated, they work hard, and the vast majority of them still underperform the market by a wide margin. Go figure!

What does all this mean for you? It means that the best strategy is to choose low-cost index funds and don't take a chance you might find something that outperforms the market with any degree of consistency. You might. But you might win the lottery too. What do think are your chances?

Some of my own personal favorite index funds for long-term goals come from Vanguard. I have been an admirer of the founder of Vanguard Funds, the late John Bogle, for many years. Founded in 1975, Vanguard is the largest provider of mutual funds in the world with over five trillion dollars (yes, that's trillion with a "t") in assets under management.

But it's important to point out that there are other low-cost, well-performing funds for you to consider as well, such as TD Ameritrade, Fidelity, Charles Schwab, and others.

A RANDOM WALK DOWN WALL STREET

Most people cannot and should not do this without outside, professional advice but, the fact is just this, you can do it on your own and save a great deal of money in fees and commissions. One of the most popular financial books of all time is "A Random Walk Down Wall Street," by Burton G. Malkiel. First published in 1973, this amazing book has sold over a million and half copies. It is filled with information and advice that is as valuable to today as it was over three decades ago!

After showing that a blindfolded monkey can pick stocks as well as any Wall Street "expert," he suggests that the only smart approach for the average investor is to select a good index fund and hang on to it. Advice that is even more prudent today than it was over forty years ago.

I highly recommend this as the SECOND most important financial book you will ever read! He has some interesting things to say about investment advisers and I think you would do well to heed his advice:

> "The problem with investment advisers is that they tend to be quite expensive and are often conflicted. Many will charge you one percent per year or more to manage your investment affairs. Brokers will frequently charge even more, costing you

two or three percent per year in fees. As I suspect we are likely to live in a single-digit investment environment for some time, such high fees will do great harm to your net investment returns.

Many investment advisers are also often conflicted. Some will put you into certain funds that give extra kickbacks to the advisers. In other words, the advisers are actually paid to distribute the funds to you. Such funds may not be in your interest (indeed, they tend to carry very high expense ratios). If you feel you must get an investment adviser, make sure that adviser is a "fee only" adviser. These advisers do not get paid for distributing investment products and thus are more likely to make decisions that are completely in your interest rather than in their interest."

Fees and commissions can destroy any gains you might otherwise have made on your investments. We are in an extended, maybe even permanent, era of low, very low interest rates. So, it is vital that you reduce costs as much as possible. As Doctor Malkiel has advised, if you must have an adviser, be sure he or she works on a fee basis only and be sure you understand what those fees are before you sign on the dotted line.

OK. So, after careful consideration, either on your own or with an adviser, you have decided which index funds are best for your Risk Ratio and you have set up your Safety Ratio at fifty-five percent in FIAs and bank accounts. Great. You can relax for now. But not for long! Because you must always be ready for rebalancing to reflect the changing circumstances of your life.

Suppose the company you've been working for goes bankrupt after you've given it twenty-five of your best, employable years. Now you face the prospect of searching for a new job to replace your lost income. How long will that take? At age fifty-five, how well will you be able to compete with much younger, equally qualified applicants for the same job? What if you must take a thirty or forty percent cut in pay if and when you do find a new job? Maybe it's time to put a far bigger percentage of your retirement savings in your safety ratio assets. Maybe it's time for a 75/25 ratio instead of 55/45.

Let's keep this scenario going. Six months after you lose your job, you finally find a different position (with a big pay cut), but you are diagnosed with a heart condition and your doctor says you need to curtail your activities and retire early. What should your ratio be now? Many people would choose 100% safety.

OK. OK. Let's not be so morbid. Let's say you are

sixty-five years old, about to retire with over $500,000 in your 401K, and you've been promising your wife for years that when you retire you would sell your house, buy a motor home and travel the country full-time. First, congrats on having built up such a nice nest egg. This puts you in the top 10% of the top 10% of all Americans. But, unless you are willing to face the prospect of an ugly divorce (and giving half of your assets to your newly minted X-wife), you have some tough decisions to make.

The Rule of 100 says your safety verses risk ratio, plus 10% because you are retired, should be 75/25, but a lot can happen in the months and years ahead and there is no way to know what circumstances might arise while you are enjoying the freedom of the road and preserving your marriage. Don't you think a ratio of 85/15 might be more prudent, at least until you and your wife get tired of traveling and decide to settle down someplace? How about 90/10? I have an idea, try this....ask your wife what she wants. I think I can guarantee it will be a long way from 75/25.

The most likely scenario that suits you will be for someone in their mid-to-late sixties or early seventies, retired and looking forward to a long and comfortable retirement. Over the years I have found that this is the time when most people are willing to forgo higher interest rates in return for more safety. At this point in your life the money you have will be all the money you will ever have. It needs to last at least as long as you do. With the possible exception of a small amount in an index fund, there are only three places I will ever recommend for your money at this stage in your life:

1. U.S. GOVERNMENT BONDS.

2. INSURED BANK ACCOUNTS.

3. ANNUITIES FROM LEGAL RESERVE LIFE INSURANCE COMPANIES.

Follow this advice and you will sleep well at night and, as an added benefit, so will I!

If you are like most people, there will come a time when virtually all your nest egg should be placed firmly in your safety ratio. Then you can relax and let the younger generations do the worrying about money, all of that will be behind you. When that happy time will be only you can decide, but I recommend that it be sooner rather than later.

SAFELY IN THE BANK

Several years ago, one of my clients, who was also a good friend and tennis buddy, asked if I would go with him to visit his eighty-one-year-old mother. He was concerned about her finances and he felt she would be more receptive to advice from me than she had been from him. So, of course I agreed, and we drove together to visit what turned out to be a very sweet lady who lived in a quiet, middle-class suburb just a few miles from my office.

After talking with her over coffee (not tea, thankfully!), I learned she had nearly six-hundred thousand dollars in her bank savings account and over a hundred thousand in her checking account. Naturally, I explained to her how having that much money not working for her, and in fact not even keeping up with inflation, was not prudent and most emphatically was not in keeping with good financial planning. She thanked me and said she would consider carefully what I had told her.

In the car driving back, my friend said he had told her basically the same thing, but she wouldn't make any changes. "What should we do?" he asked in exasperation. "We should do nothing at all," I replied. "She's comfortable with her finances and it's her money. Let her take care of it in a way that she thinks is best."

You see, in the final analysis, I believe everyone has the right to do with their money as they please. That's one of the reasons I called this book "*It's Your Money.*" Because it IS your money, and you can do as you darn well please with it. I can give you all the sound advice, all the financial theory, all the facts and figures, all the sensible reasoning in the world for taking care of it in a particular way, but YOU are always in control and you are free to do what pleases you best, however wrong and pig-headed I might think that is.

My friend's mother received comfort knowing her money was in a bank just a couple blocks from her home. In her mind, it was just sitting there waiting for her to come pick it up whenever she wanted and for whatever reason she had in her head. You and I, of course, know that her money was not sitting there in that bank. Her money had been loaned out long ago to dozens, if not hundreds, of people. If the bank did have any of her money it was on deposit with the Federal Reserve in Washington, D.C. because that's where they are required to keep their reserves. And even that would be no more than about ten percent of her deposits, if that much.

The Rule of 100 is an excellent guide to help you achieve financial security in your retirement years. But it is only a guide, you must make adjustments for your own situation, your own goals and expectations. If you are like my friend's mother, and you want to keep all your money in the bank, I'm not going to argue with you even though I cringe at the thought. Certainly, your bank will be happy to use your money and pay you practically nothing in return. Unless you have a LOT of money in the bank, let's hope you don't live too long, because inflation will keep eating away at your savings and you'll get poorer every year without even spending a dime.

Over the years I have witnessed, firsthand, how the precepts I've shared with you can be used to avoid the dangers of the stock market and create financial security and peace of mind unrivaled by other, riskier, approaches. After the great market meltdown of 2007/2008, I received dozens of calls from worried clients concerned that they may have lost their money just like their friends, relatives and millions of other Americans. It gave me great pleasure to assure them they had not lost a single dime.

I do not look forward to the next great financial crisis. But I know this for sure, when it comes, and history assures us it most certainly will come, those who take my advice, and follow the strategies laid out in this book, will fare infinitely better than those who do not. The choice is yours.

EPILOGUE

A FINAL WORD

OK. It's your turn now. I've done my part by bringing you this knowledge, I can do no more. It's up to you to put these things to work for you to help secure your own financial future. By reading this book, you now know more about financial history and safe money concepts than most of the "experts" you see on television, hear on the radio, or deal with personally.

We have covered quite a bit of territory together in these pages. We have looked at the long history of money, that strange and powerful human construct which down through the long ages has evolved into NOTHING!

We traveled back in time to learn the history of banking and Wall Street, the center of world capitalism (at least for now).

We examined the long and honorable history of annuities issued by the most stable, most trusted financial institutions in the world, legal reserve life insurance companies. We learned why annuities should be a part of the financial strategies of anyone over age fifty who is concerned about the safety of their money.

In the first chapter of this book, I told you my goal was to, *"speak to you in plain English about important financial subjects in an easy-to-read, understandable, non-threatening format, without a bunch of technical gobblede-goop"*. Looking back over these pages, almost two years after I began writing them, I'm not at all sure I've managed to attain that goal. But I've done the very best I can. I leave it to you to determine the degree of my success, or failure.

Since I plan to continue working for many years to come, I may have the opportunity to meet with you sometime. You may catch one of my radio broadcasts or you might even attend one of my financial workshops. GREAT! You can let me know personally what you think of my book (please be kind).

I never attempt to impress my religious views on anyone else. I believe we all have the God-given right to practice our own faith, as we see it, and to the best of our ability. Having said that, I also believe we are all children of the same God and we are on this earth for a reason. There is purpose to our lives. I believe life itself is a wonderful gift. It is incumbent upon us all to make the most of this gift, treasuring each day as another pearl in the long string of pearls that makes up the totality of our lives.

So, enjoy your life!

Be happy,

Be healthy.

Live long and live well.

Take care of yourself and take care of your family. Be kind and generous to those whose fate has placed them at a lower place in life and in more difficult circumstances than your own.

And take care of your finances, my friend. Always remember that you can't get rich quickly, but you can sure get poor faster than you can blink your eyes! How well you handle financial matters will have a major impact on the quality of your life and the lives of your loved ones for the rest of your life.

So please, follow the guidelines presented in this book. Be very conservative and very careful how you invest and who you trust for advice.

Because after all;

IT'S YOUR MONEY!

Best wishes to you and your family.

                        J. Sylvester Wood

Luke 17:20-21